COVID SOCIETIES

COVID Societies presents a compelling and accessible overview of key sociocultural theories that can help us make sense of the diverse, dynamic and complex elements of the COVID crisis. These include discussions of the political economy perspective; biopolitics; risk society and cultures; gender and queer theory; and more-than-human theory. The book provides insights into everyday life around the world as people battled with containing the pandemic and explores the broader historical, social, cultural and political contexts in which these responses have developed.

COVID-19 is the most serious pandemic to affect the world in the past century. We have all lived in 'COVID societies', the long-term effects of which have yet to be experienced or imagined. The COVID crisis has affected countries, regions within countries and social groups within regions in strikingly different ways. These impacts are continually changing, just as the novel coronavirus has mutated into different strains and variants. Throughout the book, a series of intertwined threads cross back and forth between the macropolitical and micropolitical dimensions of COVID-19: contagion, death, risk, uncertainty, fear, social inequalities, stigma, blame and power relations. Overarching these threads are five complementary themes: the historicity of COVID societies; the tension between local specificities and globalising forces; the control and management of human bodies;

the boundary between Self and Other; and the continuously changing sociomaterial environments in which the world is living with and through the shocks of the COVID crisis.

This book will be of great interest to anyone seeking to understand the manifold complex sociocultural consequences of the COVID-19 pandemic.

Deborah Lupton is SHARP Professor in the Faculty of Arts, Design & Architecture, University of New South Wales (UNSW) Sydney, Australia. Her research is interdisciplinary, spanning sociology, communication and cultural studies. She is located in the Centre for Social Research in Health and the Social Policy Research Centre and leads both the Vitalities Lab and the UNSW Node of the Australian Research Council Centre of Excellence for Automated Decision-Making and Society. She is an elected Fellow of the Academy of the Social Sciences in Australia and holds an Honorary Doctor of Social Science degree awarded by the University of Copenhagen.

COVID SOCIETIES

Theorising the Coronavirus Crisis

Deborah Lupton

LONDON AND NEW YORK

Cover image: © Ashkan Forouzani

First published 2022
by Routledge
4 Park Square, Milton Park, Abingdon, Oxon OX14 4RN

and by Routledge
605 Third Avenue, New York, NY 10158

Routledge is an imprint of the Taylor & Francis Group, an Informa business

© 2022 Deborah Lupton

The right of Deborah Lupton to be identified as author of this work has been asserted in accordance with sections 77 and 78 of the Copyright, Designs and Patents Act 1988.

All rights reserved. No part of this book may be reprinted or reproduced or utilised in any form or by any electronic, mechanical, or other means, now known or hereafter invented, including photocopying and recording, or in any information storage or retrieval system, without permission in writing from the publishers.

Trademark notice: Product or corporate names may be trademarks or registered trademarks, and are used only for identification and explanation without intent to infringe.

British Library Cataloguing-in-Publication Data
A catalogue record for this book is available from the British Library

Library of Congress Cataloging-in-Publication Data
Names: Lupton, Deborah, author.
Title: COVID societies: theorising the coronavirus crisis/Deborah Lupton.
Description: Abingdon, Oxon; New York, NY: Routledge, 2022. |
Includes bibliographical references and index. |
Identifiers: LCCN 2021048172 (print) | LCCN 2021048173 (ebook) |
ISBN 9781032060552 (hbk) | ISBN 9781032060569 (pbk) |
ISBN 9781003200512 (ebk)
Subjects: LCSH: COVID-19 (Disease)–Social aspects. |
COVID-19 (Disease)–Economic aspects. |
COVID-19 (Disease)–Political aspects. | Interdisciplinary research.
Classification: LCC RA644.C67 L87 2022 (print) |
LCC RA644.C67 (ebook) | DDC 362.1962/414–dc23/eng/20211220
LC record available at https://lccn.loc.gov/2021048172
LC ebook record available at https://lccn.loc.gov/2021048173

ISBN: 978-1-032-06055-2 (hbk)
ISBN: 978-1-032-06056-9 (pbk)
ISBN: 978-1-003-20051-2 (ebk)

DOI: 10.4324/9781003200512

Typeset in Bembo
by Newgen Publishing UK

CONTENTS

Introduction: COVID societies   1

1 COVID in context: histories and narratives of health, risk and contagion   14

2 The macropolitics of COVID: a political economy perspective   36

3 The biopolitics of COVID: Foucauldian approaches   59

4 Risk and COVID: risk society and risk cultures   82

5 Queering COVID: insights from gender and queer theory   102

6 More-than-human COVID worlds: sociomaterial perspectives   124

Conclusion: reflections on COVID futures   146

Index   *152*

INTRODUCTION
COVID societies

On 11 March 2020, the Director-General of the World Health Organization (WHO), Dr Tedros Adhanom Ghebreyesus, gave a media briefing where he formally announced that the global outbreak of a new infectious disease, COVID-19, should be characterised as a pandemic. He went on to state that pandemic 'is not a word to use lightly or carelessly. It is a word that, if misused, can cause unreasonable fear, or unjustified acceptance that the fight is over, leading to unnecessary suffering and death'. Adhanom Ghebreyesus also observed that the COVID-19 pandemic was the first to be caused by a novel coronavirus (SARS-CoV-2) and called for countries to 'take urgent and aggressive action' to contain the spread of the virus as quickly as possible (World Health Organization, 2020a).

As Adhanom Ghebreyesus' dramatic words suggest, when pandemics erupt, societies are flung into a crisis that goes well beyond health and medical impacts. The COVID pandemic is much more than a health emergency. In an extremely short space of time, the spread of the novel coronavirus across the world has led to massive challenges and disruptions to everyday life and livelihoods globally.

This book provides a compelling and accessible overview of key sociocultural theories that can help us make sense of the diverse, dynamic and complex elements of the COVID crisis, which began in the first days of the new year of 2020. References to relevant findings from empirical research and vivid examples of social, cultural and political responses to the pandemic internationally are provided in each

DOI: 10.4324/9781003200512-1

of the book's chapters to illustrate the application of these theoretical perspectives. The book provides insights into what experiences of the first year and a half of this global crisis was like across the regions of the world as they battled with containing COVID, acknowledging the broader contexts in which these responses have developed.

The COVID crisis is suffused with discourses, practices and emotions related to people's reactions to risk and uncertainty. The world has changed so dramatically since January 2020 that some social theorists are now referring to the current period as 'the Virocene Epoch' (Fernando, 2020). Whether this time of global disaster will come to be seen as a new epoch remains to be seen. However, there is no doubt that we are all currently living in 'COVID societies': the long-term effects of which have yet to be experienced or imagined. I refer to 'societies' in the plural because there is no singular SARS-CoV-2; hence there is no individual COVID society. Despite the short history of the COVID crisis, we can already see how rapidly social institutions and social relations have changed during this time. The crisis has affected countries, regions within countries and social groups within regions in strikingly different ways. These impacts are continually changing, just as the novel coronavirus is constantly mutating into different strains and variants.

A constellation of expert knowledges has developed around monitoring, communicating, managing and predicting COVID risk. These knowledges are comprised of government and non-government policies, medical, public health and social research, journalistic reporting, apps for mobile devices, online dashboards on health organisation websites, mathematical modelling of future scenarios and the processing, announcement and display of a multitude of vital metrics (numbers of COVID cases, people infectious while in the community, hospitalisations, deaths, recoveries, people in quarantine, vaccines injected and so on). The dragging on of the crisis and the dynamic nature of peaks and troughs in COVID case numbers, together with sudden outbreaks and the emergence of new variants of SARS-CoV-2, have meant that predictions about the future, official modelling, 'road maps' and government policies for ways out and the re-institution of some kind of 'normality' are constantly subject to change – in some cases on an hourly or daily basis. Throughout the crisis, plans for everyday life have continually been disrupted, making it difficult to establish any kind of certainty.

The first cases of COVID-19 (then an unidentified disease caused by an unknown pathogen) were reported on 30 December 2019 in the Chinese city of Wuhan. The official name for this novel coronavirus as SARS-CoV-2 (severe acute respiratory syndrome coronavirus type 2) and the disease it causes as COVID-19 (a contraction of coronavirus disease 2019) was announced by WHO on 11 February 2020 (World Health Organization, 2020b). While the outbreak already looked extremely serious by March 2020, it became apparent over the course of the year and into 2021 that the spread of SARS-CoV-2 was going to be difficult to contain. By late September 2020, one million COVID deaths had been confirmed. By July 2021, the confirmed global COVID death toll had reached 4 million. At this point in the pandemic, the USA had reported the highest number of confirmed COVID deaths (one in seven of the global toll), followed by Brazil (where official figures were considered to be far below the real count for that country). Of the top ten countries with the highest official death rates, eight were from Latin America and the Caribbean (Aljazeera, 2021; The Lancet, 2021).

New highly effective vaccine platforms capable of protecting people from serious illness and death from COVID, and to some extent, infection from the novel coronavirus, have been quickly developed. These vaccines are the first ever invented to be effective against severe coronavirus disease. Remarkably, the initial range of vaccines was invented, tested, approved and deployed within a mere nine months following the official declaration of COVID as pandemic. The first mass vaccination programme against COVID started in December 2020, after months of intense and ground-breaking work by virologists and pharmaceutical companies. By May 2021, at least 13 vaccines had been administered globally, developed by the Pfizer/BioNTech, AstraZeneca/Oxford, Johnson & Johnson, Moderna and the China National Biotec Group companies (World Health Organization, 2021c). However, throughout 2021, most of the world's populations (and particularly those in the Global South) struggled to gain access to these vaccines, due to lack of supply, poor supporting infrastructure, vaccine refusal or hesitancy among citizens or a combination of all these factors.

By mid-2021, many countries were experiencing second, third or even fourth waves of the pandemic, with a new, more contagious strain of SARS-CoV-2, the Delta variant, rapidly spreading. Countries that in the first year had successfully suppressed the pandemic, such as Indonesia, India, Australia, New Zealand and some African countries, were dealing with new or worse COVID outbreaks. Nations in the South-East Asian region that had until this time been relatively unscathed by the pandemic, including Vietnam, Malaysia, Myanmar and Thailand as well as Pacific Island nations such as Papua New Guinea and Fiji, were also battling serious outbreaks.

Like most other people worldwide, it was through mainstream news media reporting that I first became aware of a new infectious disease outbreak in China in the early days of January 2020. Due to my academic background involving decades of social research and theorising about topics related to medicine, public health, embodiment and risk, I soon realised that this outbreak could be more momentous than initial reporting in the Western news media had led publics to believe. In addition to my initial background in sociology and biological anthropology, I hold a Master of Public Health degree, which gave me some training in applied public health approaches such as epidemiology. Following this degree, I built on my interests in the sociology and anthropology of medicine and public health by completing a doctorate that involved a critical discourse analysis of the reporting of HIV/AIDS in the Australian press, which was later published as *Moral Threats and Dangerous Desires: AIDS in the News Media* (Lupton, 1994). Since then, I have conducted many empirical studies and applied sociocultural theory to a diverse array of health-, medical- and risk-related topics and issues, including the books *Medicine as Culture* (Lupton, 2012), *The Imperative of Health* (Lupton, 1995), *The New Public Health* (Petersen & Lupton, 1996), *Television, AIDS And Risk* (Tulloch & Lupton, 1997), *Food, the Body and the Self* (Lupton, 1996), *Risk* (Lupton, 2013), *Risk and Everyday Life* (Tulloch & Lupton, 2003), *Fat* (Lupton, 2018) and *Digital Health* (Lupton, 2017).

All this previous scholarship has contributed to my current work on the sociocultural and political dimensions of the COVID crisis. Following WHO's official declaration of the COVID outbreak as a pandemic, I embarked on a COVID-focused research programme. I began with editing a special section of the *Health Sociology Review* journal on the topic of 'Sociology and the Coronavirus (COVID-19) Pandemic' (Lupton, 2020). I then co-edited *The COVID-19 Crisis: Social Perspectives* volume (Lupton & Willis, 2021) with contributors from North America, Australia, Europe, the UK, South Africa and New Zealand. My chapter published in this book provided an overview of the historical and sociocultural contexts in which the COVID pandemic erupted (Lupton, 2021). I went on to co-author a monograph on the sociomaterial dimensions of face masks in the COVID era (Lupton et al., 2021) and a series of journal articles and book chapters reporting findings from empirical research about people's experiences of the early months of the pandemic (Downing et al., 2021; Lupton & Lewis, 2021a, 2021b, 2022; Watson et al., 2021a, 2021b).

Building on and extending this line of scholarship, on both the previous health and medical issues and the current pandemic, I show throughout this book that COVID societies are complex, situated and dynamic. Existing socioeconomic disadvantage, marginalisation and stigmatisation have been exacerbated by the COVID crisis, and nationalism has come to the fore. Given these intensely sociocultural, economic and political dimensions, the COVID crisis has been described not only as a 'pandemic' but also as a 'syndemic' (Irons, 2020). Syndemic is a term first used by anthropologist Merrill Singer (2009) to encapsulate the bio-social combination of illnesses and diseases and other vulnerabilities that interact synergistically to render a disease outbreak even more serious in certain social groups or populations. It was soon discovered by public health and social researchers that in the case of the COVID crisis, these factors include older age, race and ethnicity, geographical location, poverty, working and housing conditions, poor healthcare services and pre-existing illnesses or impairments.

In this book, I will devote attention to the historical antecedents, discourses, narratives and imaginaries as well as the material practices that contribute to contemporary responses to the current pandemic. While SARS-CoV-2 is a new pathogen and COVID-19 is a new disease, significant elements of their sociocultural and political as well as their health impacts are rooted in the past. The words and discourses employed when discussing illness, disease and risk play a crucial role in shaping how people with infectious diseases are portrayed and treated by others. The discursive modes which Wald (2008) terms 'outbreak narratives' and Dey and Lynteris (2021) describe as 'pandemic imaginaries' have been perpetuated in popular cultural portrayals across a range of previous epidemics and pandemics.

The COVID crisis has entered the world as part of a continuing stream of increasingly frequent new and emerging infectious diseases. After the devastating Spanish influenza pandemic of 1918–1919, there was a hiatus of 40 years in which no major epidemics of new diseases occurred. However, since the 1950s, and particularly since the turn of the twenty-first century, numerous novel pathogens have erupted that are believed to have passed to humans from animal hosts or reservoirs and then mutated so that human-to-human transmission became possible, leading to an epidemic (localised outbreak) or pandemic (global outbreak). Such diseases are therefore described as 'zoonotic', with the pathogen most often spread from birds or mammals, including domesticated and wild animals (Jia et al., 2021).

Table I.1 shows the new diseases that have emerged over the hundred years since the Spanish influenza pandemic, providing details of the estimated numbers of deaths resulting from each outbreak. There are several issues to consider when viewing this simple table. One is that the metrics provided of the death toll for each outbreak can only ever be estimates. Measuring deaths and their causes relies on complicated systems of identification and reporting that are variable across historical periods and between countries or even regions within countries. For example, incomplete reporting is one reason for why the numbers of deaths from Spanish influenza globally is such a broad estimate, with a range of 20 to 50 million (Kavey & Kavey, 2020).

It has already been claimed that the numbers of confirmed deaths from the COVID pandemic are massively unreported, due to official statistics not being adequately gathered in many low-income countries as a result of politically based decisions, or sheer lack of resources to collect and analyse these data. The COVID mortality figure of 5.4 million in Table I.1, taken from WHO's regularly updated online dashboard showing confirmed COVID cases and deaths globally and by country, is probably much lower than the real metric. WHO's dashboard relies on the numbers reported to it by the health agencies in individual countries. A different metric – valuations of excess COVID deaths across countries – has demonstrated the extent of the increase in loss of life due to the pandemic. Across Europe and in South Africa, the USA and Latin America, for example, the death toll from COVID has been far greater than usual expected mortality figures (The Economist, 2021).

It is notable that of the serious disease outbreaks listed in Table I.1, only some received intense media attention at the time: but these were not necessarily the outbreaks with the highest death tolls. This observation points to another key feature of infectious disease outbreaks: how much public attention and news coverage they receive and the tenor of this coverage in terms of suggestions about the threat the outbreak poses. Due to a combination of complex sociocultural and political

TABLE I.1 Timeline of major epidemics and pandemics since the Spanish influenza pandemic

Date	Disease and virus	Number of deaths
1918–1919	Spanish influenza (H1N1)	20–50 million
1956–1958	Asian influenza (H2N2)	2 million
1968–1970	Hong Kong influenza (H3N2)	1 million
1981 onwards	HIV/AIDS (human immunodeficiency syndrome/acquired immunodeficiency syndrome)	37 million★
2003 onwards	Avian influenza (H5N1) 'bird flu'	455★
2003–2004	SARS (severe acute respiratory syndrome/SARS-CoV)	774
2009–2010	Pandemic influenza (H1N1) 'swine flu'	152,000–575,000
2012 onwards	MERS (Middle East respiratory syndrome/MERS-CoV)	858★
2014–2016	Ebola virus disease	11,325
2015–2017	Zika virus disease	Not fatal
2019 onwards	COVID-19 (coronavirus disease 2019/SARS-CoV-2)	5.4 million★

★As of 29 December 2021.

Sources: Centers for Disease Control and Prevention, 2021; National Institute of Allergy and Infectious Diseases, 2021; World Health Organization, 2021.

factors, some of these outbreaks have received much more heightened affective responses of fear and panic than others, even when mortality rates are comparatively low. Zika virus disease, for example, is not fatal and generally causes only mild symptoms in those who are infected. However, this disease can cause a serious birth defect (microcephaly, or under-development of the foetal brain) if a pregnant woman contracts the pathogen. Zika virus disease has attracted news media attention primarily because of these effects on infants (Kavey & Kavey, 2020; Ribeiro et al., 2018).

Meanwhile, other serious pandemics that have caused tens of millions of deaths globally, and continue to kill large numbers of people in some parts of the world, rarely receive attention. The most compelling example of such a pandemic is the Spanish influenza outbreak of 1918–1919, which has been estimated to be the deadliest pandemic in history. Yet in recent years it has also often been characterised as the 'forgotten' pandemic; its effects were overshadowed by the terrible loss of life in and social upheavals of World War I and its aftermath (Chandra et al., 2020). HIV/AIDS provides a more recent example. As shown in Table I.1, this disease has caused tens of millions of deaths worldwide. While HIV/AIDS has become well-controlled in high-income countries due to advances in drugs to prevent and treat the disease, it is still rampant in sub-Saharan Africa, where hundreds of thousands of deaths occur each year (World Health Organization, 2021d). HIV/AIDS received high levels of news coverage in the first decade of its emergence, when it was severely affecting some social groups in the Global North, and public health authorities were warning that it could quickly spread across populations if preventive actions were not taken (Lupton, 1994; Watney, 1987). However, since the 1990s, HIV/AIDS as a major health problem is rarely discussed in public forums or the news media in the Global North.

A key focus of this book is on identifying the narratives, imaginaries, practices and feelings concerning risks and uncertainties that pervade COVID societies, as the spread of SARS-CoV-2 and its variants continues to wreak havoc around the world. Publics' understandings and practices related to COVID risks and uncertainties draw on expert sources but also rely on people's lived experiences and knowledge of previous infectious diseases, their affective and multisensory embodied responses and their engagements with other people, both in-person and online. The phenomena of the virus known as SARS-CoV-2 and the disease known as COVID-19 are constantly changing: so too, people's understandings, practices, feelings and experiences are evolving. Governments' and health agencies' responses are also adapting to new COVID conditions in this ever-changing pandemic landscape. As I show throughout the book, all these resources, knowledge, affective forces and things come together to form dynamic assemblages of risk, contagion, health, recovery or containment in relation to the COVID crisis.

This book

As I show throughout this book, there is no single or 'correct' way to analyse the sociocultural and political dimensions of a phenomenon as forceful and fluid as the COVID crisis. Various lenses can be applied, each of which offer a different perspective on what is a complicated and unpredictable catastrophe that is continuing to evade the attempts of policymakers, government agencies, public health experts, global health peak bodies and medical science to control it. Bringing a range of different perspectives to bear to understand the impact of COVID and people's everyday experiences of living through the crisis offers a multidimensional perspective, shining the spotlight in turn on the complicated facets that comprise the phenomenon that is the continuing COVID catastrophe.

Chapter 1 addresses histories and narratives of health, risk and contagion in relation to COVID societies. This chapter provides the sociocultural and political contexts into which SARS-CoV-2 entered in the tail end of 2019. This part of the discussion draws on the writings of medical historians, sociologists, anthropologists and cultural geographers who have identified the responses to earlier serious infectious diseases such as the plague, Spanish influenza and the series of new viral epidemics and pandemics that have emerged since that deadly outbreak a century ago. I then trace the unfolding of the COVID-19 outbreak from its very beginnings as it came into the awareness of health authorities, first in Wuhan and then worldwide, including the crucial first 100 days of the pandemic and ensuing developments.

The next five chapters are each devoted to a specific theoretical approach that can be used to offer insights into the multifaceted dimensions of COVID societies. Chapter 2 adopts a macropolitical perspective, drawing on foundational Marxian scholarship together with feminist critiques, critical disability studies, critical race theory and postcolonial theory to demonstrate how a political economy approach can be applied to the COVID crisis. The concepts of medical dominance, the social determinants of health and globalisation are explained. The chapter documents how marginalised and disadvantaged social groups and populations have experienced the crisis, often in ways that have entrenched and exacerbated social inequalities. The discussion in this chapter also considers how neoliberal and capitalist economic systems have contributed to the socioeconomic catastrophes emerging as SARS-CoV-2 spread around the world and, in some cases, have even profited from the crisis.

Chapter 3 brings together macropolitical and micropolitical perspectives in engaging with Foucauldian approaches to biopolitics. I begin with an overview of Michel Foucault's scholarship on the three forms of power: sovereign power, disciplinary power and biopower. Applications of these modes of power in relation to medicine and public health are discussed, including commentary on the tensions between caring for the self and the protection of the body politic. The scholarship of philosophers Giorgio Agamben and his concepts of bare life and states of exception, Roberto Esposito and his notions of affirmative biopolitics and immunitary mechanisms, and Achille Mbembe and his writings on necropolitics is also outlined. This discussion is followed by an account of Foucauldian viewpoints on the biopolitical dimensions of COVID societies, including discussion of how these theorists analysed social and governmental responses to the crisis.

Concepts and practices of risk in COVID times are the focus of detailed analysis in Chapter 4. The writings of Ulrich Beck on risk society and Mary Douglas' insights in her scholarship on risk cultures are explained. Beck offers a critical sociological perspective in developing his concepts of reflexive modernisation, individualisation and cosmopolitanism in the context of late modernity and what he characterises as world risk society. Douglas' anthropological scholarship on risk focuses on the symbolic boundaries between Self and Other that are configured when cultures respond to concepts of risk and danger. Each of these theoretical positions is evaluated for what they can offer for understanding how COVID societies and cultures have emerged and changed as the pandemic has continued.

Chapter 5 introduces insights from scholarship in gender and queer theory and demonstrates how they can be productively applied to an analysis of embodiment, affect and socialities in COVID times. As I show, COVID has queered everyday human experience; in turn, queer theory can be applied to queer COVID. The major precepts of these intertwined bodies of literature are explained, with reference to the influential scholarship of philosophers such as Mel Chen, Michel Foucault, Judith Butler, Elizabeth Grosz, Gilles Deleuze, Félix Guattari and Julia Kristeva. The contribution of such interdisciplinary fields of study as queer necropolitics, queer death studies, crip theory, fat studies and critical animal studies and how they operate to challenge binary oppositions and norms of embodiment and identity are discussed. The concepts from this scholarship are then applied to the COVID crisis, challenging the taken-for-granted assumptions and norms of behaviour that have dominated mainstream COVID narratives and imaginaries.

Chapter 6, the final substantive chapter, builds on previous chapters by devoting further attention to the material-discursive dimensions of

COVID. The insights offered by the more-than-human perspectives espoused in non-Western philosophies, particularly Indigenous and First Nations cosmologies, together with the feminist materialism scholarship of Western philosophers Karen Barad, Rosi Braidotti, Donna Haraway and Jane Bennett are presented. Such an approach broadens the One Health perspective that positions human health as intertwined with ecological health. More-than-human scholarship highlights the vibrant forces, connections and agencies that are generated with and through people's encounters with other living creatures, spaces and the objects within spaces. The analysis in the chapter focuses on the capacities that have been both opened and closed by more-than-human COVID assemblages, including those generating capacities for good health, recovery and well-being.

I finish this book with offering some reflections on how post-COVID societies might be established that offer greater possibilities for both human and non-human flourishing. As I write in the brief Conclusion chapter, given the complexities and transformations in human experience we have already experienced globally, the futures of COVID societies remain difficult to predict. What is certain is that the 'old normal' way of life in COVID societies across the globe cannot and should not be re-established. As we learn to live with and through COVID, we must work towards better conditions for people across geographical regions and cultures. Taking our cue from Indigenous/First Nations cosmologies in acknowledging our vulnerability and using this knowledge to better care for the more-than-human worlds in which we are emplaced is a way forward to care more deeply about ourselves and our fellow species.

References

Aljazeera. (2021). Global COVID deaths hit 4 million amid rush to vaccinate. www.aljazeera.com/gallery/2021/7/8/global-covid-deaths-hit-4-million-amid-rush-to-vaccinate

Centers for Disease Control and Prevention. (2021). www.cdc.gov/

Chandra, S., Christensen, J., & Likhtman, S. (2020). Connectivity and seasonality: the 1918 influenza and COVID-19 pandemics in global perspective. *Journal of Global History*, 15(3), 408–420.

Dey, I., & Lynteris, C. (2021). On 'pandemic imaginary': an interview with Christos Lynteris. *Society and Culture in South Asia*, 7(1), 175–180.

Downing, L., Marriott, H., & Lupton, D. (2021). "'Ninja' levels of focus": therapeutic holding environments and the affective atmospheres of telepsychology during the COVID-19 pandemic. *Emotion, Space and Society*, *40*. https://doi.org/10.1016/j.emospa.2021.100824

Fernando, J. L. (2020). The Virocene Epoch: the vulnerability nexus of viruses, capitalism and racism. *Journal of Political Ecology*, *27*(1), 635–684.

Irons, R. (2020). Pandemic … or syndemic? Re-framing COVID-19 disease burden and 'underlying health conditions'. *Social Anthropology*, *28*(2), 286–287.

Jia, P., Dai, S., Wu, T., & Yang, S. (2021). New approaches to anticipate the risk of reverse zoonosis. *Trends in Ecology & Evolution*, *36*(7), 580–590.

Kavey, R.-E. W., & Kavey, A. B. (2020). *Viral Pandemics: From Smallpox to COVID-19*. Routledge.

Lupton, D. (1994). *Moral Threats and Dangerous Desires: AIDS in the News Media*. Taylor & Francis.

Lupton, D. (1995). *The Imperative of Health: Public Health and the Regulated Body*. Sage.

Lupton, D. (1996). *Food, the Body and the Self*. Sage.

Lupton, D. (2012). *Medicine as Culture: Illness, Disease and the Body* (3rd ed.). Sage.

Lupton, D. (2013). *Risk* (2nd ed.). Routledge.

Lupton, D. (2017). *Digital Health: Critical and Cross-Disciplinary Perspectives*. Routledge.

Lupton, D. (2018). *Fat* (2nd ed.). Routledge.

Lupton, D. (2020). Special section on 'Sociology and the Coronavirus (COVID-19) Pandemic'. *Health Sociology Review*, *29*(2), 111–112.

Lupton, D. (2021). Contextualising COVID-19: sociocultural perspectives on contagion. In D. Lupton & K. Willis (Eds.), *The COVID-19 Crisis: Social Perspectives* (pp. 14–24). Routledge.

Lupton, D., & Lewis, S. (2021a). 'The day everything changed': Australians' COVID-19 risk narratives. *Journal of Risk Research*, online first. https://doi.org/10.1080/13669877.2021.1958045

Lupton, D., & Lewis, S. (2021b). Learning about COVID-19: a qualitative interview study of Australians' use of information sources. *BMC Public Health*, *21*(1). https://doi.org/10.1186/s12889-021-10743-7

Lupton, D., & Lewis, S. (2022). Coping with COVID-19: the sociomaterial dimensions of living with pre-existing mental health illness during the early stages of the coronavirus crisis. *Emotion, Space & Society*, *42*. https://doi.org/10.1016/j.emospa.2021.100860

Lupton, D., Southerton, C., Clark, M., & Watson, A. (2021). *The Face Mask in COVID Times: A Sociomaterial Analysis*. De Gruyter.

Lupton, D., & Willis, K. (Eds.). (2021). *The COVID-19 Crisis: Social Perspectives*. Routledge.

National Institute of Allergy and Infectious Diseases. (2021). www.niaid.nih.gov/

Petersen, A., & Lupton, D. (1996). *The New Public Health: Health and Self in the Age of Risk*. Sage.

Ribeiro, B., Hartley, S., Nerlich, B., & Jaspal, R. (2018). Media coverage of the Zika crisis in Brazil: the construction of a 'war' frame that masked social and gender inequalities. *Social Science & Medicine, 200*, 137–144.

Singer, M. (2009). *Introduction to Syndemics: A Critical Systems Approach to Public and Community Health*. John Wiley & Sons.

The Economist. (2021). Tracking COVID-19 excess deaths across countries. *The Economist*. www.economist.com/graphic-detail/coronavirus-excess-deaths-tracker

The Lancet. (2021). COVID-19 in Latin America – emergency and opportunity. *The Lancet, 398*(10295). https://doi.org/10.1016/S0140-6736(21)01551-8

Tulloch, J., & Lupton, D. (1997). *Television, AIDS and Risk: A Cultural Studies Approach to Health Communication*. Allen & Unwin.

Tulloch, J., & Lupton, D. (2003). *Risk and Everyday Life*. Sage.

Wald, P. (2008). *Contagious: Cultures, Carriers, and the Outbreak Narrative*. Duke University Press.

Watney, S. (1987). The spectacle of AIDS. *October, 43*, 71–86.

Watson, A., Lupton, D., & Michael, M. (2021a). The COVID digital home assemblage: transforming the home into a work space during the crisis. *Convergence, 178*(1), 136–150.

Watson, A., Lupton, D., & Michael, M. (2021b). Enacting intimacy and sociality at a distance in the COVID-19 crisis: the sociomaterialities of home-based communication technologies. *Media International Australia, 178*(1), 136–150.

World Health Organization. (2020a). WHO Director-General's opening remarks at the media briefing on COVID-19 – 11 March 2020. www.who.int/director-general/speeches/detail/who-director-general-s-opening-remarks-at-the-media-briefing-on-covid-19--11-march-2020

World Health Organization. (2020b). Timeline: WHO's COVID-19 response. www.who.int/emergencies/diseases/novel-coronavirus-2019/interactive-timeline?gclid=CjwKCAiA17P9BRB2EiwAMvwNyGWSa7LCiCAgb9r1TIgGmjmcYnZzOj7_zVA80ZeeVZyUsfqM35BvrhoCofQQAvD_BwE#event-7

World Health Organization. (2021c). Coronavirus disease (COVID-19): vaccines. www.who.int/news-room/q-a-detail/coronavirus-disease-(covid-19)-vaccines?topicsurvey=v8kj13)&gclid=Cj0KCQjwweyFBhDvARIsAA67M71umtGXFWis_UHtkLuthIIhg2jFLjYIrMNctYlEg7Cqb9aeZoRldbUaAoFLEALw_wcB

World Health Organization. (2021d). Number of deaths due to HIV/AIDS. *World Health Organization*. www.who.int/data/gho/data/indicators/indicator-details/GHO/number-of-deaths-due-to-hiv-aids

World Health Organization. (2021e). www.who.int/

1
COVID IN CONTEXT

Histories and narratives of health, risk and contagion

Introduction

Contagious disease outbreaks have presented serious challenges globally throughout recorded history, with continuing recurrences of influenza, cholera, plague, typhus, smallpox and yellow fever (Bashford, 2016; Kavey & Kavey, 2020; Mack, 1991). Recent evolutionary genetic research has identified DNA evidence that humans in East Asia were encountering coronavirus infections more than 20,000 years ago (Souilmi et al., 2021). Along with inspiring fear and dread about threats to human health, major new or recurring infectious disease outbreaks are always accompanied by significant sociocultural and political disruptions and transformations. These crises often call into question ways of viewing and living in the world, as well as exposing and entrenching forms of social discrimination and inequalities.

This chapter provides an overview of the historical, sociocultural and political contexts of the COVID-19 crisis. Medical historians, sociologists, anthropologists and cultural geographers have shown that social, cultural and political responses to the emergence or return of deadly pathogens often bring to the surface hidden, unacknowledged or long-established beliefs and practices. The chapter demonstrates how these perspectives have offered much of value in relation to the analysis of the sociocultural and political dimensions of previous serious infectious diseases. This discussion is followed by an account of how the new virus SARS-CoV-2 and the new disease COVID-19 emerged in the early months of 2020 and developments in the pandemic throughout 2020 and into 2021.

Changing concepts of health, risk and contagion

Many of the responses and experiences we have felt and seen in COVID societies harken back to previous infectious disease outbreaks. Concepts concerning health, risk, disease and contagion play a significant role in how societies and cultures configure pandemic narratives and imaginaries and conduct their everyday lives accordingly. These concepts have changed dramatically in Western cultures since the Enlightenment. Ideas about human bodies and disease have shifted significantly even within the past century, incorporating centuries-old ideas as well as bringing in new ideas from other cultures or introduced by scientific or medical discoveries about the body.

In societies of the Global North in the contemporary era, people are encouraged to see themselves as a continuing unfinished project, requiring work and effort to shape and improve, seeking to impose order and certainty upon what is perceived to be a chaotic, uncertain, disorderly world. The role of fate and chance in structuring people's life opportunities and well-being is repudiated. Instead, it is believed that most aspects of life are malleable and amenable to the exertion of will. As I argued in my book *Risk* (Lupton, 2013), in Western societies, the belief prevailing in pre-Enlightenment times that dangers and catastrophes are caused by fate or supernatural forces has given way to the conviction that these phenomena are often human-made and that someone or some organisation can be identified and held responsible. Nonetheless, much older understandings of embodiment and risk sometimes re-emerge and can be identified in pandemic narratives and imaginaries, including contemporary responses to the COVID crisis.

The notion of the 'civilised' body, emerging in early modern Europe, is particularly important to contemporary Western understandings about the ideal body. The civilised body is understood to be that which is self-controlled, which is autonomous and self-regulated. Its boundaries are kept contained from the outside world and from others. In contrast to this ideal notion is the 'grotesque' or 'uncivilised' body, the body that lacks self-control and self-discipline and is constantly breaching its boundaries. The body that is suffering pain or illness, that is deformed or disabled, that is dying, tends to conform far more closely to the 'grotesque' body than to the civilised body (Shilling, 1993).

Cultural theorist Susan Sontag (1990) wrote about the contemporary moral meanings of illness in her influential essays 'Illness as metaphor' and 'AIDS and its metaphors'. She observed that there is a long history of punitive approaches to disease and that: 'Nothing is more punitive than to give a disease a meaning – that meaning being invariably a moralistic one' (Sontag, 1990, p. 58). Sontag gave the example of the figure of the leper in medieval times: individuals whose outward signs of fleshly decay were believed to be displaying their internal corruption, and who were therefore shunned and relegated to the outskirts of communities or kept in special facilities well away from townspeople. This meaning lives on today in the simile describing people being treated 'like a leper': that is, socially excluded for reasons that may not be related to health.

Ideas about the human body and its relationship to the social and physical environment in pre-Enlightenment eras in Europe drew on the natural philosophy of the ancient Greeks and Romans. The 'humoral' model positioned disease as caused by imbalances between the four humours (blood, black bile, yellow bile and phlegm) and the four elements (air, earth, water and fire), as well as influenced by 'nonnaturals': exercise, food, drink, sexual activity, sleep and frame of mind or affective state (Hartnell, 2018; Lupton, 2012). It was thought that illness and disease in the form of foul vapours, or 'miasmas', entered the body through the skin and bodily orifices. Therefore, medieval Europeans believed that the body could best be protected against such vapours by wrapping it in tightly woven clothing, reinforcing the 'closed' nature of the body. Carrying fragrant herbs was another way that people sought to avoid the odours they believed caused disease (Vigarello, 1990).

Systematic public health measures for the containment and control of the plague were introduced from the fourteenth century, which remain part of infectious disease control today. These measures include cleaning of odorous places or those believed to be infected, contact tracing, restrictions on movement, closing of borders and identifying certain social groups (usually the most disadvantaged) as more contagious and contaminating than others. Quarantine as a way of managing infectious disease outbreaks has been traced back to medieval and early modern European approaches to controlling leprosy and bubonic plague from the twelfth century by enforcing a 40-day period of isolation on all travellers (the word quarantine comes from the Italian for this length of time) (Bashford, 2016). These practices were based on the observation that disease could be airborne and that the sharing of space and place and people having close contact with each other could spread disease; even if it was not initially understood that microorganisms were involved in this infectious process (Newman, 2012; Pamuk, 2007). The first recorded use of the term 'pandemic' (from the Greek 'pan' meaning all and 'demos' meaning people) was by English physician Gideon Harvey in 1666. He used the term 'pandemick' interchangeably with 'epidemick' to describe a malignant disease that 'haunt[ed] a Country' (Honigsbaum, 2009, p. 1939).

Bubonic plague, or 'the Black Death', provides a compelling example of the social upheavals that pandemics can leave in their wake. Several regions of the world were devastated by recurring major outbreaks of bacterial bubonic plague over 400 years between the fourteenth and early eighteenth centuries, with the pathogen spreading from Central Asia into Europe by way of vast trade routes. It is believed that the Black Death was so named because of the darkened appearance of the painful swellings, or buboes, that appeared in the lymph nodes in the groin area of its victims' bodies, as well as their blackened extremities from gangrene (Totaro, 2011). It has been estimated that one third of the population of western Europe died from it between 1348 and 1350. Plague outbreaks also contributed to economic depression due to the death of agricultural workers and tradespeople as well as the disruption of trade and regular major dislocations of urban populations. These changes in turn led to social reforms, such as the decline in feudalism, an increase in wages for the workers who survived, and eventually the Renaissance (Newman, 2012; Pamuk, 2007).

Strict quarantine measures were implemented in England in the late sixteenth century in response to recurring plague outbreaks. Parishes in afflicted areas were required to institute and enforce household quarantine and establish public 'pesthouses', where people who had been exposed to plague cases, together with members of their households, were kept inside. People were forcibly isolated in their houses, with doors padlocked by officials, painted with a large red cross and emblazoned with the words 'Lord have mercy upon us'. By law, watchmen were stationed outside, to ensure that no one entered or left the house. People who did break quarantine were dealt with harshly by the law because of the threat they posed to the public health. These people tended to be from the lower social orders, while wealthy people escaped this level of scrutiny and policing and in some cases were able to escape the pestilent city to seek refuge in the country (Newman, 2012).

Writings during the times of plague – or 'plague literature' – recounted the terror of living through these waves of outbreaks. The plague was used as a metaphor for cultural and moral degeneration, afflicted societies thereby deserving God's punishment, or imagined utopian futures where the lessons of the plague would inspire better societies (Totaro, 2011). Accounts such as Daniel Defoe's *A Journal of the Plague Year*, published in 1722 but referring to the plague of 1665, vividly depicted the feelings of horror and desperation that were part of living in plague times in England, including the physical suffering of those afflicted, the near collapse of social order, massive burial pits heaped with the dead bodies of plague victims, the intense threats posed by having any contact with other people and the importance of physical isolation to ensure survival (Lau, 2016). The cultural resonances of the plague remain in contemporary Western societies. For example, we talk of being 'plagued' by a problem and Shakespeare's line from his play *Romeo and Juliet*, 'A plague on both your houses', is a well-known epithet today.

Even in these early times, quarantine was a controversial approach for the effects it had not only on people's health but on their psychological and economic well-being, as well as signalling 'problem' social groups or populations as requiring stringent measures of discipline and containment (Bashford & Strange, 2003). Despite the growing evocation of the discourses of scientific authority to justify traditional preventive measures such as quarantine, the contagion narratives and practices employed into the twentieth century often went beyond simple disease containment and moved into highly political and symbolic realms. Used in later eras, quarantine frequently became a way for nations to position the Other as contaminated by virtue of their potential contagion. This portrayal frequently was associated with nationalist, colonial and racist sentiments about the bodies of non-white peoples. In the newly federated nation of Australia in the early twentieth century, for example, quarantine practices and policies contributed to the concept of the 'pure' nation that required protection from pathologised non-white Others to achieve cohesion and good health (Bashford, 1998).

It was only a century ago that the Spanish influenza pandemic killed tens of millions of people worldwide. The influenza virus causing this pandemic, believed to be of avian origin, was extremely infectious and had a high mortality rate due to secondary bacterial pneumonia that afflicted those who become ill. It was named the Spanish influenza because a Madrid newspaper was the first to report the outbreak, but it is unlikely that the virus originated in Spain. Indeed, medical historians now suggest that the virus developed on a farm in the US state of Kansas, spreading quickly from there via the post-World War I rapid movements of populations across the globe using networks of steamships and railway lines. Due to these mass mobilities, the virus causing Spanish influenza infected an estimated 500 million people – approximately one third of the world's population – and killed at least 20–50 million people worldwide (Chandra et al., 2020; Kavey & Kavey, 2020).

There was far less understanding of how viral pathogens operated and spread in 1918–1919. Scientific medicine was just beginning to learn how to control the risks of infection from viruses and bacteria. It was known that basic hygiene measures and quarantine were effective in controlling the spread of pathogens, but exactly what they were and how they affected the body, or how to treat the disease they caused, was not yet understood (Kavey & Kavey, 2020). There were no possibilities for testing people for infection, providing antibiotics to treat the secondary bacterial infection or developing effective vaccines to protect them against the pathogen (Oldstone, 2014). Medical equipment such as respirators to effectively assist with breathing difficulties and drug therapies had not yet been developed to effectively treat respiratory disease (Kavey & Kavey, 2020).

Viruses were first isolated and their role in disease identified at the very end of the nineteenth century. It was not until the 1930s that electron microscopes powerful enough to detect viruses were developed, and until the 1940s that cell cultures to grow them came into use. Vaccines against viral infections and anti-viral therapies of the type that have transformed HIV/AIDS from a deadly disease to a chronic illness (at least in wealthy countries, if not in sub-Saharan Africa) only began to emerge in the mid-to-late twentieth century (Oldstone, 2014). In the 1940s and 1950s, concepts of health in American society tended to represent the body as a castle or fortress, with distinct openings that required protection from external invaders. Following the mid-nineteenth century sanitary reform movement in England and the USA, hygiene became a dominant strategy for defending the body from the 'germs' that sought to enter through its orifices and subsequently cause disease. During the 1960s and 1970s, however, the notion of the body as harbouring an interconnected immune system developed, drawing on changing scientific medical knowledge about immune response (Martin, 1994). The human body was portrayed in immunological discourses as a metaphorical nation-state requiring protection against the 'invasion' of pathogens. The immune system was depicted in similarly militarist terms as mounting a battle, fought by white blood cells against the pathogens (Martin, 1990).

These imaginaries of contagion, risk and immunity continue to be used in relation to COVID, as the following chapters will detail. However, there is also a growing body of research on the human microbiome (the constellation of microorganisms that live on and in the human body) that has identified the beneficial interdependencies of humans with microorganisms in generating states of shared good health. Many species of microorganisms are essential parts of the body's ecologies. Scientific research has found that people's encounters with microorganisms from birth onwards play a major role in the development of their immune system and support the optimal functioning of their digestive system and good skin health through establishment of colonies of 'good bacteria' (Young, 2017). These understandings of the microbiome have implications for how people are beginning to conceptualise the role of microorganisms such as viruses and bacteria in supporting human health and immunity rather than simply posing a threat as pathogens attacking the body (Greenhough et al., 2020).

Epidemics and pandemics since the Spanish influenza outbreak

Despite the devastation of the Spanish influenza pandemic, for much of the twentieth century public health authorities and agencies became rather complacent about the threat that infectious disease outbreaks posed to global health. Developments such as better knowledge about infectious disease causes and containment had led to improved sanitation systems and hygiene programmes, as well as the mass rollout of vaccination programmes: all of which contributed to reducing infection cases and deaths. Once scientific medicine had developed better knowledge about viruses and vaccines, devastating outbreaks of infectious diseases became well controlled for a time. The global elimination of smallpox was achieved, together with a significant reduction in disease and mortality from diseases such as measles, poliomyelitis, rubella, yellow fever, mumps, cancers caused by human papilloma virus and seasonal influenza in countries that were able to implement mass childhood vaccination campaigns (Oldstone, 2014).

As shown in the table presented in the Introduction chapter, Asian influenza killed approximately 2 million people between 1956 and 1958, which was followed by Hong Kong influenza outbreak of 1968–1970, accounting for the deaths of an estimated 1 million more. However, by the 1970s, it appeared that widespread infectious diseases were largely under control (Arrizabalaga, 2016). In 1981, WHO announced in its 'Global Strategy for Health For All by the Year 2000' that it aimed to prevent the spread of the most infectious diseases by the end of the twentieth century (World Health Organization, 1981). Attention consequently turned to the prevention and control of 'lifestyle' non-communicable diseases and conditions such as cardiovascular disease, high blood pressure, cancer and Type II diabetes and persuading people to change their everyday behaviours to avoid these illnesses or an early death (Lupton, 1995).

The advent of HIV/AIDS cases in 1981 was a shocking awakening to the reality that new infectious diseases were still emerging and posing a global threat: including to wealthy countries. June 2021 marked 40 years since the first public health agency reporting (the US Centers for Disease Control) of a cluster of cases of rare pneumonia and Kaposi's sarcoma, a rare form of cancer, among young gay men in the US city of Los Angeles. For many years, HIV/AIDS had an extremely high mortality rate because HIV, the virus causing AIDS, attacked the immune system, leaving the body open to opportunistic infections that could not easily be fought off. However, HIV/AIDS infections and deaths have been significantly reduced in some countries since the mid-1990s, with the development of effective pre-exposure prophylactic drugs and antiretroviral therapy for those already infected that can reduce it to a chronic condition rather than a fatal disease. From the early 1980s, AIDS activists had engaged in sustained advocacy and protests to force the US government to increase the pace of the development of antiretroviral drugs and make them more affordable (Ryan, 2021).

While these drugs have been more readily available for people living with HIV in wealthy countries, they remain in short supply for those in low-income countries. HIV/AIDS therefore remains a serious health concern in parts of the world. HIV is transmitted through unprotected sex, particularly for men who have sex with men, and sharing needles to inject drugs. These activities remain stigmatised in many countries and prevention and treatment efforts have been limited in countries where they are illegal or where HIV exposure, transmission or non-disclosure are criminalised (The Lancet, 2021a). It has been estimated that HIV/AIDS has killed more than 37 million people worldwide since 1981, with a total over 75 million HIV infections. Today, HIV/AIDS is still causing many deaths, particularly in sub-Saharan Africa: in 2020, an estimated 680,000 people died from HIV-related illnesses (World Health Organization, 2021b). As I observed in the Introduction chapter, however, very little news media attention in the Global North has been devoted to these fatalities. Once HIV/AIDS became well controlled in wealthy countries, it largely dropped off the agenda as a newsworthy topic.

With the emergence of HIV/AIDS and the continuing threat it poses to some parts of the world, the assumption that emerging infectious diseases would be readily controlled was challenged. In response to these concerns, in 1994 WHO created a programme on emerging infectious diseases (Arrizabalaga, 2016). During the 1990s, commentators were beginning to announce warnings of the 'next major pandemic' they predicted would devastate the world – most probably transmitted from an animal host. The outbreak narrative referring to 'emerging' (or novel) infections began to be used in the popular media, news reporting and public health circles alike. These narratives referred to a changing world in which pathogens that could affect humans were moving into densely populated regions by way of the processes of globalisation (Wald, 2008). Bestselling non-fiction popular books on this topic included Richard Preston's *The Hot Zone* and Laurie Garrett's *The Coming Plague*, both published in 1994.

Another well-known product of this genre is the 2011 Hollywood film *Contagion*. In this film, a new deadly virus originating in Hong Kong causing a pandemic is only one of the villains of the story. The narrative is filled with selfish and careless people who spread the virus with little regard for the health or safety of others (Davis, 2017). The heroes of this and several other pandemic films (e.g., the 1995 film *Outbreak*) are typically scientists such as virologists working to develop a vaccine and public health experts such as epidemiologists and contact tracers, seeking desperately to identify the source of infection and discover a way of halting the pandemic in its tracks. Meanwhile, societies are rapidly descending into civil unrest and mayhem, as panic grows. Cities are placed under lockdown, and panic buying, looting and violence eventuate (Lynteris, 2016; Wald, 2008).

Despite these popular narratives expressing frightening warnings of impending health and societal threats posed by new infectious diseases, since the turn of the twenty-first century complacency has characterised most wealthy countries' approaches to pandemic preparedness. Many populations and governments of high-income countries began to view emerging infectious disease outbreaks as phenomena that only affect other places in the world. Postcolonial and low-income countries in particular were positioned as the primary sites of contagion. It was assumed that in these locations, hygiene standards, healthcare systems and public health regulations were inferior and that humans living there were engaging in closer and more frequent interactions with the types of animals that are hosts for new zoonotic viruses (Irons, 2020).

Since 2000, however, the world has seen a growing number of new pathogens causing disease in humans, including both influenza viruses and coronaviruses. Outbreaks of avian influenza ('bird flu'), SARS, pandemic influenza ('swine flu'), MERS, Ebola virus disease and Zika virus disease have all occurred since 2003 (refer to Table 1 in the Introduction chapter for further details). The original SARS coronavirus (SARS-CoV-1), believed to originate from bats, with civets as the reservoir species, was first reported in Asia in February 2003. More than 8,000 people worldwide became ill with severe acute respiratory syndrome (SARS), the disease caused by SARS-CoV-1, and 774 deaths were reported (National Institute of Allergy and Infectious Diseases, 2020). The SARS outbreak only lasted six months: no new cases have been reported since 2004. However, the initial speed of travel of this coronavirus to 29 countries, territories and areas generated great levels of concern from public health officials and agencies at the time. This outbreak eventually was relatively easy to control because people who were infected with this coronavirus were not highly infectious until days after their symptoms emerged and could therefore be easily identified and isolated from others (Anderson et al., 2004).

Another coronavirus (MERS-CoV) emerged in 2012. MERS (Middle East respiratory syndrome), spread from camels but possibly originating in bats, was first reported in the Middle East in 2012, with 80% of cases identified in that region despite some spread to 27 countries. While cases continue to be identified, with a known death count of 858 by mid-2021, MERS-CoV is not highly contagious and has therefore not sparked a pandemic (National Institute of Allergy and Infectious Diseases, 2020; World Health Organization, 2021a).

In 2009, there was short-lived alarm about the outbreak of pandemic influenza ('swine flu') in the Global North: particularly as it was a new strain of the same highly infectious virus (H1N1) that caused the Spanish influenza pandemic. The swine influenza outbreak received saturation news coverage in a news environment that had become far more interconnected throughout the twentieth century, assisted by the introduction of online news reports with rolling updates (Davis et al., 2014). WHO formally declared a public health emergency of international concern in April 2009 and characterised this H1N1 outbreak as officially a pandemic in June 2009. Grave fears were held for a time about this influenza outbreak, particularly as it seemed to be primarily affecting younger people and pregnant women, as did the Spanish influenza pandemic. The swine influenza pandemic was estimated to have infected at least 1.4 billion people, causing 152,000 to 575,000 deaths globally. However, it was quickly controlled, probably because many older people already had immunity to it following previous exposure to similar viruses. An effective new vaccine was soon developed to prevent infections in other groups. In August 2010, WHO declared that this pandemic was over. H1N1 now circulates as a cause of seasonal influenza, with new vaccines developed each year to combat it. Nevertheless, it was largely believed by public health authorities that this was a lucky miss (Davis & Lohm, 2020).

Since the swine influenza scare, increasingly forceful calls have been made by public health experts to improve global pandemic preparedness, with at least 11 high-level panels and commissions publishing specific recommendations to that effect. These recommendations often suggested that WHO needed to strengthen its role as the leading coordinating global organisation and that its funding should therefore be increased. One outcome of these recommendations was the establishment of a new WHO Health Emergencies Programme in 2016. However, most recommendations were never implemented, as the threat posed by pandemics was continually underplayed by WHO Member States, in favour of attention to controlling and managing the risks of war, terrorism, nuclear disaster or global financial insecurity (The Independent Panel for Pandemic Preparedness & Response, 2021).

The emergence and spread of SARS-CoV-2 and COVID-19

COVID-19 erupted 16 years after the decline of the original SARS pandemic. This second version of the SARS coronavirus – SARS-Cov-2 – has proven to be far less easy to contain. SARS-CoV-2 and the hundreds of other coronaviruses that currently circulate (which include SARS-CoV-1, MERS and the common cold as well as many coronaviruses that affect animals) owe their name to the 'corona' of spike proteins on their surface (National Institute of Allergy and Infectious Diseases, 2021). The novel coronavirus spreads in a similar way to most influenza viruses: via contaminated droplets and aerosols (microscopic droplets) emitting from the nose and mouth of infected people when they sneeze, cough, sing, laugh, speak or breathe heavily, or by touching objects on which such particles may settle (World Health Organization, 2020a). Measures to prevent against infection are similar for SARS-CoV-2 and influenza: hand and cough hygiene (frequent hand washing, using tissues, coughing into the elbow), face coverings, not standing too close to other people and vaccination. Some initial symptoms are also similar for both diseases: principally fever, headache, cough, body aches and fatigue (Sample, 2021).

Some variants of SARS-CoV-2 that have emerged, including the Delta strain which caused new outbreaks in 2021, are more contagious than most influenza viruses. A notable characteristic of the first variants of COVID at least was that up to 40% of people who become infected displayed no or only very mild symptoms or were infectious before they develop symptoms and therefore could transmit the pathogen without realising that they had it (National Institute of Allergy and Infectious Diseases, 2020). COVID is a more lethal disease than the types of influenza viruses that are now considered seasonal. As a comparison, an estimated 44,505 people died in England from seasonal influenza during three combined annual flu seasons from 2015 to 2019, while COVID killed the same number in England during the first nine weeks of 2021 alone (Sample, 2021).

At its most serious, COVID not also causes severe respiratory illness but can also affect many other organs and systems in the body, including causing multiple organ failure that then leads to death (Centers for Disease Control and Prevention, 2021). Those most at risk from serious COVID and death are older people or people with preexisting serious health conditions (Centers for Disease Control and

Prevention, 2021). Another major problem is the risk of developing 'long COVID' for those who have become infected with SARS-CoV-2. Even if the COVID symptoms are mild, infection can result in a series of prolonged symptoms such as breathlessness, headaches and extreme fatigue that can continue for many months after the initial infection (Sudre et al., 2021).

The time elapsing from the first reporting of a cluster of cases of a new respiratory disease that was later to be named 'COVID-19' to the first million confirmed cases worldwide was slightly less than one hundred days. The World Health Organization (WHO) has published a timeline of how events unfolded from the very beginning of the first observation of a cluster of unusual cases of atypical pneumonia in the Chinese city of Wuhan, Hubei province (World Health Organization, 2020b). The Independent Panel for Pandemic Preparedness & Response (2021) also put together a chronological account of the events unfolding between late 2019 and the end of March 2020, by which time the SARS-CoV-2 had spread extensively around the world. Co-chaired by former Prime Minister of New Zealand Helen Clark and former President of Liberia Ellen Johnson Sirleaf and published in May 2021, this report is scathing, noting that most countries were woefully unprepared for containing and managing the SARS-CoV-2 outbreak (The Independent Panel for Pandemic Preparedness & Response, 2021). The Panel concluded that these months were characterised by some evidence of early and rapid action by nations and global health authorities but delay, hesitation to act decisively and denial of the threat were also prevalent in their responses. The events and developments outlined below in these first one hundred days of the COVID crisis are synthesised from these two chronologies.

On 30 December 2019, the first cases of 'atypical viral pneumonia of unknown cause' who had been admitted to hospitals in Wuhan in the Chinese province of Hubei were reported in two urgent notices to hospital networks in the city by officials from the Wuhan Municipal Health Commission. Wuhan clinicians noted that several of these atypical pneumonia patients had visited the same 'wet market' in that city. At that market, live sea creatures and other animals were sold for human consumption, suggesting it was a key source of transmission. The following day, a Chinese business publication published a report on one of these notices, which in turn was picked up by several disease surveillance system operating in the region. WHO's Headquarters office in Geneva was alerted to the report. Later that day, the Wuhan Municipal Health Commission sent out a bulletin for public notice, reporting that 27 cases of this disease had been identified.

By the end of December 2019, it seemed likely from the epidemiology of these Wuhan cases that human-to-human transmission of this as yet unidentified and unnamed pathogen was likely. The WHO Country Office in China requested further information from the Wuhan officials on 1 January 2020, activating its Incident Management Support Team as part of its emergency response framework. By 2 January, the Wuhan Institute of Virology had sequenced almost the entire genome of the novel virus. There were 44 reported cases by 3 January. WHO released a tweet about this Wuhan pneumonia cluster (which had not yet caused any deaths) on 4 January, noting the investigations to determine the cause were underway. It released its first Disease Outbreak News report on 5 January about these cases. All countries were warned to take precautions against the spread of this new virus. On 9 January, Chinese authorities had determined that the pathogen was a novel coronavirus, similar to the pathogen SARS-CoV that had caused the disease known as SARS. Chinese scientists had developed a first test for the virus by 10 January.

The first death from infection with this novel coronavirus was reported by the China media on 11 January. The first case outside China was reported in Thailand on 13 January and a second case in Japan on 16 January: both cases had travelled from Wuhan. Chinese health experts publicly announced on 20 January that the virus was transmissible between humans and that healthcare workers had become infected. Wuhan officials had instituted a city-wide lockdown on 23 January in the attempt to control the spread. At this point in the outbreak, 830 cases and 25 deaths had been reported. The first case outside Asia was recorded in the USA on 21 January and the first European cases (a total of three) were reported by France on 24 January. WHO's first mission to Wuhan to investigate the outbreak took place on 20–21 January 2020. It declared a 'public health emergency of international concern' on 30 January: the organisation's highest level of alarm.

At this point in the outbreak, this new virus, first referred to as '2019 novel coronavirus', had begun to spread quickly around the world. A total of 98 cases had been detected in 18 countries. By 4 February, over 20,000 confirmed cases and 425 deaths had been reported in China, and 176 cases in 24 other countries. One week later, WHO announced that the novel coronavirus would be named SARS-CoV-2 and the disease it caused referred to as COVID-19. By 7 March, over 100,000 confirmed cases of COVID-19 had been reported globally. The outbreak was officially declared as a pandemic by WHO on 11 March 2020, when reported cases had reached over 118,000 across 114 countries. By 13 March, Europe had become the epicentre of the pandemic, with more reported cases and deaths than the rest of the world combined, apart from China.

On 4 April 2020, almost 100 days after the first Wuhan cases had been reported, WHO reported that over 1 million confirmed cases had been notified worldwide, with the pace of infection rapidly increasing. Even at that stage, many countries' governments worldwide had not yet taken decisive action to contain the spread of the virus. WHO's declaration on 30 January of a 'public health emergency of international concern' was largely ignored. Only a minority of countries began comprehensive prevention and response strategies. Many countries did very little throughout the month of February, even while cases were rapidly spreading and climbing globally. Most governments either did not appreciate the seriousness of the threat posed by COVID-19 or wanted to take a 'wait-and-see' approach rather than implement significant action. Due to their previous experiences with the SARS pandemic, several east and south-east Asian countries were among the earlier responders, while African countries who had been through the Ebola threat also learned from this and put measures into place quickly. Many other countries did not spring into action until they noted the exponential rise in cases and rapid spread of the virus. Serious actions that could have contained such a huge expansion in cases and deaths were implemented too late.

The news media have played a crucial role in informing people about COVID. The outbreak was reported in the news media from the first days of the emergence of the cases in Wuhan. In many cases, news media coverage was vital in helping people learn about this mysterious new disease and providing an outlet for warnings, updates, restrictions and prevention advice from health experts and government authorities. It took several weeks for the news media in the Global North to position the new infectious disease outbreak in Wuhan as a problem that might be relevant outside China. My investigation of the first month of reporting in Australian online news outlets (Lupton, 2021) found that journalists tended to frame the threat as a problem like

SARS: specific to China or Asia and therefore posing a minimal risk to Australians. Similarly, in the first three months of the pandemic, news media in the USA focused on the emergence of the outbreak and its spread into different regions of the world, as well as on the social and economic effects. There was less attention paid in these reports to the health risks posed by the outbreak to Americans (Hubner, 2021). In China itself, in the space of the first month of the outbreak the media framed COVID as initially conquerable at a local (Wuhan city) level but then as a catastrophic national (Chinese) risk, then finally becoming represented as a global crisis (Wang & Mao, 2021).

Since the first one hundred days period of the COVID crisis, epicentres have changed, and subsequent waves of outbreaks have been experienced in many countries. One hundred million COVID cases had been reported by the end of January 2021 – just over a year since the first infections had been recorded. By mid-2020, the USA was leading the world in numbers of COVID cases and deaths (Tanne, 2020). A year later, however, the situation was very different. Case numbers were declining in the USA, Canada and most of Europe but surging in Latin America and Asia, with most countries in these regions (with the exception of China) going through second, third or fourth waves of the pandemic (Toole et al., 2021). In May 2021, a second exponential wave of infections was overwhelming India, which was recording world records of numbers of cases recorded daily. By June 2021, the Delta variant of the virus was spreading through countries such as the UK, sparking new waves of infection.

Despite the effects of the Delta variant, by mid-2021 – 18 months since the emergence of the first cases – COVID vaccination programmes had begun to make a major impact on how well the disease had been controlled in different countries and regions. Wealthy countries, including Israel, the UAE, Chile, the UK, the USA, Hungary, Iceland, Denmark and Singapore, had achieved high vaccination levels per capita (over 50 doses per 100 citizens) (The Visual and Data Journalism Team, 2021), which resulted in steep declines in numbers of infections and deaths from COVID in most of those countries (Toole et al., 2021). In most of Asia and the Pacific region, however, a sense of complacency deriving from early successful management and containment of SARS-CoV-2 spread and, in some cases, continued isolation from the rest of the world, led to governments failing to secure enough vaccines or effectively rolling them out in mass immunisation programmes.

While countries in the northern hemisphere with high levels of their populations fully vaccinated were beginning to open to foreign travel, Australia's and Japan's international borders remained closed. Sporadic sudden regional lockdowns were still being instituted in Australia as well as in China and Thailand to contain new outbreaks of coronavirus infection. Japan was battling a fourth wave of infection even as it was hosting the Summer Olympic Games in Tokyo, which had already been delayed by a year due to the pandemic. In Vietnam, Thailand and Taiwan, mass vaccination programmes had hardly been established by June 2021, while Australia, New Zealand, China, Hong Kong, Japan, Indonesia and South Korea were not managing to reach high levels of vaccinations in their populations due to problems with vaccine supply, vaccine hesitancy, complacency or low motivation on the part of their citizens to seek immunisation (Cave, 2021).

According to WHO, the continent of Africa 'experienced its worst pandemic week ever' in early July 2021, with major increases in cases driven by the Delta variant. Sixteen African countries reported a resurgence of infections, with new case counts doubling every 18 days across the continent. A third wave of infection was affecting countries mainly in southern and eastern Africa and Tunisia was going through a fourth wave. Uganda, which previously had controlled the spread of the coronavirus well, was experiencing a surge in infections. Across these African countries, healthcare systems were stretched to breaking point, and medical supplies such as testing kits and vaccines were nowhere near required levels. In a continent with 1.3 billion people, only around 54 million COVID tests had been conducted and only 53 million vaccine doses administered, with only 1% of the population fully vaccinated (Dahir, 2021). Countries in Latin America and the Caribbean were struggling with the spread of several new COVID variants and limited vaccine supplies simultaneously with widespread political crises, civil unrest and loss of trust in governments (The Lancet, 2021b).

There is continuing uncertainty about how the SARS-CoV-2 pathogen first came to move from animals to infecting humans. The initial hypothesis was that a bat species may have been a host reservoir for the virus. WHO convened a technical mission of experts who travelled to China to investigate the conditions under which the virus broke out there and reported its findings in March 2021. However, consensus has not yet been reached about SARS-CoV-2's exact origin and how and when it first moved from an animal host to a human and when human-to-human transmission began. The mission's report suggested that SARS-CoV-2 may have already been circulating outside China towards the end of 2019 before the first cases had been reported in Wuhan (World Health Organization, 2021c).

Concluding comments

In this chapter, I have outlined some of the key historical, social, cultural and political dimensions of concepts of risk, health, contagion and disease and detailed how societies have responded to previous epidemics and pandemics. I have provided an overview of the emergence of COVID, emphasising how little prepared many countries in the Global North particularly were to prepare for and manage the new pathogen SARS-CoV-2, despite a foundation of experience and expert knowledges on which they could have drawn.

As was argued in the Independent Panel for Pandemic Preparedness & Response's report (2021, p. 20), despite sustained warnings from national and global health agencies and authorities that the emergence of a highly infectious new virus of zoonotic origin was highly likely, 'COVID-19 exposed a yawning gap between limited, disjointed efforts at pandemic preparedness and the needs and performance of a system when actually confronted by a fast-moving and exponentially growing pandemic'. Chapter 2, which presents a political economy perspective, expands the discussion of these macropolitical dimensions of the COVID crisis and the ever-growing divide between wealthy and less socioeconomically advantaged social groups and world regions as they struggled to confront the challenges posed by the pandemic.

References

Anderson, R. M., Fraser, C., Ghani, A. C., Donnelly, C. A., Riley, S., Ferguson, N. M., Leung, G. M., Lam, T. H., & Hedley, A. J. (2004). Epidemiology, transmission dynamics and control of SARS: the 2002–2003 epidemic. *Philosophical Transactions of the Royal Society of London. Series B: Biological Sciences*, *359*(1447), 1091–1105.

Arrizabalaga, J. (2016). The global threat of (re) emerging diseases: contesting the adequacy of biomedical discourse and practice. In J. E. Davis & A. M. Gonzalez (Eds.), *To Fix or to Heal: Patient Care, Public Health, and the Limits of Biomedicine* (pp. 177–207). New York University Press.

Bashford, A. (1998). Quarantine and the imagining of the Australian nation. *Health*, *2*(4), 387–402.

Bashford, A. (Ed.) (2016). *Quarantine: Local and Global Histories*. Palgrave Macmillan.

Bashford, A., & Strange, C. (2003). Isolation and exclusion in the modern world. In A. Bashford & C. Strange (Eds.), *Isolation: Places and Practices of Exclusion* (pp. 1–21). Routledge.

Cave, D. (2021). Why Asia, the pandemic champion, remains miles away from the finish line. *The New York Times*. www.nytimes.com/2021/06/15/world/asia/asia-coronavirus.html?smid=tw-share

Centers for Disease Control and Prevention. (2021). Similarities and differences between flu and COVID-19. www.cdc.gov/flu/symptoms/flu-vs-covid19.htm

Chandra, S., Christensen, J., & Likhtman, S. (2020). Connectivity and seasonality: the 1918 influenza and COVID-19 pandemics in global perspective. *Journal of Global History*, *15*(3), 408–420.

Dahir, A. L. (2021). Africa marks its 'worst pandemic week' yet, with cases surging and vaccine scarce, the WHO says. *The New York Times*. www.nytimes.com/2021/07/08/world/africa-coronavirus-cases-who.html?smid=em-share

Davis, M. (2017). "Is it going to be real?" Narrative and media on a pandemic. *Forum Qualitative Sozialforschung/Forum: Qualitative Social Research*, *18*(1). www.qualitative-research.net/index.php/fqs/article/view/2768

Davis, M., & Lohm, D. (2020). *Pandemics, Publics, and Narrative*. Oxford University Press.

Davis, M., Lohm, D., Flowers, P., Waller, E., & Stephenson, N. (2014). "We became sceptics": fear and media hype in general public narrative on the advent of pandemic influenza. *Sociological Inquiry*, *84*(4), 499–518.

Greenhough, B., Read, C. J., Lorimer, J., Lezaun, J., McLeod, C., Benezra, A., Bloomfield, S., Brown, T., Clinch, M., D'Acquisto, F., Dumitriu, A., Evans, J., Fawcett, N., Fortané, N., Hall, L. J., Giraldo Herrera, C. E., Hodgetts, T., Johnson, K. V.-A., Kirchhelle, C., Krzywoszynska, A., Lambert, H., Monaghan, T., Nading, A., Nerlich, B., Singer, A. C., Szymanski, E., & Wills, J. (2020). Setting the agenda for social science research on the human microbiome. *Palgrave Communications*, *6*(1). https://doi.org/10.1057/s41599-020-0388-5

Hartnell, J. (2018). *Medieval Bodies: Life, Death and Art in the Middle Ages*. Profile Books.

Honigsbaum, M. (2009). Pandemic. *The Lancet*, *373*(9679), 1939.

Hubner, A. (2021). How did we get here? A framing and source analysis of early COVID-19 media coverage. *Communication Research Reports*, *38*(2), 112–120.

Irons, R. (2020). Pandemic … or syndemic? Re-framing COVID-19 disease burden and 'underlying health conditions. *Social Anthropology*, *28*(2), 286–287.

Kavey, R.-E. W., & Kavey, A. B. (2020). *Viral Pandemics: From Smallpox to COVID-19*. Routledge.

Lau, T. C. W. (2016). Defoe before immunity: a prophylactic *Journal of the Plague Year*. *Digital Defoe: Studies in Defoe & His Contemporaries*, 8(1), 23–39.
Lupton, D. (1995). *The Imperative of Health: Public Health and the Regulated Body*. Sage.
Lupton, D. (2012). *Medicine as Culture: Illness, Disease and the Body* (3rd ed.). Sage.
Lupton, D. (2013). *Risk* (2nd ed.). Routledge.
Lupton, D. (2021). A 'mystery SARS-like illness'. How did Australian news outlets cover the COVID-19 outbreak when it first emerged in early 2020? *Medium*. https://deborahalupton.medium.com/its-been-a-year-since-the-first-australian-covid-19-cases-d7e4df44a550
Lynteris, C. (2016). The epidemiologist as culture hero: visualizing humanity in the age of "the next pandemic". *Visual Anthropology*, 29(1), 36–53.
Mack, A. (1991). *In Time of Plague: The History and Social Consequences of Lethal Epidemic Disease*. NYU Press.
Martin, E. (1990). Toward an anthropology of immunology: the body as nation state. *Medical Anthropology Quarterly*, 4(4), 410–426.
Martin, E. (1994). *Flexible Bodies: Tracking Immunity in American Culture from the Days of Polio to the Age of AIDS*. Beacon Press.
National Institute of Allergy and Infectious Diseases. (2020). COVID-19, MERS & SARS. www.niaid.nih.gov/diseases-conditions/covid-19
National Institute of Allergy and Infectious Diseases. (2021). Coronaviruses. www.niaid.nih.gov/diseases-conditions/coronaviruses
Newman, K. L. (2012). Shutt up: bubonic plague and quarantine in early modern England. *Journal of Social History*, 45(3), 809–834.
Oldstone, M. (2014). History of virology. *Encyclopedia of Microbiology*. www.ncbi.nlm.nih.gov/pmc/articles/PMC7150144/
Pamuk, Ş. (2007). The Black Death and the origins of the 'Great Divergence' across Europe, 1300–1600. *European Review of Economic History*, 11(3), 289–317.
Ryan, B. (2021). How antiretrovirals transformed the HIV epidemic: a timeline. *POZ*. www.poz.com/article/antiretrovirals-transformed-hiv-epidemic-timeline
Sample, I. (2021). Why living with Covid would not be the same as flu. *The Guardian*. www.theguardian.com/world/2021/jul/05/why-living-with-covid-would-not-be-the-same-as-flu
Shilling, C. (1993). *The Body and Society*. Sage.
Sontag, S. (1990). *Illness as Metaphor and AIDS and Its Metaphors*. Anchor Books.
Souilmi, Y., Lauterbur, M. E., Tobler, R., Huber, C. D., Johar, A. S., Moradi, S. V., Johnston, W. A., Krogan, N. J., Alexandrov, K., & Enard, D. (2021). An ancient viral epidemic involving host coronavirus interacting genes more than 20,000 years ago in East Asia. *Current Biology*, 31(16), 3504–3514.
Sudre, C. H., Murray, B., Varsavsky, T., Graham, M. S., Penfold, R. S., Bowyer, R. C., Pujol, J. C., Klaser, K., Antonelli, M., & Canas, L. S. (2021). Attributes and predictors of long COVID. *Nature Medicine*, 27(4), 626–631.

Tanne, J. H. (2020). Covid-19: US sees record rise in cases. *British Medical Journal, 370*. www.bmj.com/content/370/bmj.m2676.abstract

The Independent Panel for Pandemic Preparedness & Response. (2021). *COVID-19: Make It the Last Pandemic*. https://theindependentpanel.org/wp-content/uploads/2021/05/COVID-19-Make-it-the-Last-Pandemic_final.pdf

The Lancet. (2021a). 40 years of HIV/AIDS: a painful anniversary. *The Lancet, 397*(10290). https://doi.org/10.1016/S0140-6736(21)01213-7

The Lancet. (2021b). COVID-19 in Latin America – emergency and opportunity. *The Lancet, 398*(10295). https://doi.org/10.1016/S0140-6736(21)01551-8

The Visual and Data Journalism Team. (2021). Covid map: coronavirus cases, deaths, vaccinations by country. *BBC News*. www.bbc.com/news/world-51235105

Toole, M., Umali, S., van Gemert-Doyle, C., & Majumdar, S. (2021). *COVID-19 Global Trends and Analyses. Volume 1, May 2021*. https://burnet.edu.au/system/asset/file/4695/5.1.1-May-Global-Update-Vol-1-COVID-19-Epi-and-trends.pdf

Totaro, R. (2011). Introduction. In R. Totaro & E. B. Gilman (Eds.), *Representing the Plague in Early Modern England* (pp. 1–25). Routledge.

Vigarello, G. (1990). *Concepts of Cleanliness: Changing Attitudes in France since the Middle Ages*. Cambridge University Press.

Wald, P. (2008). *Contagious: Cultures, Carriers, and the Outbreak Narrative*. Duke University Press.

Wang, D., & Mao, Z. (2021). From risks to catastrophes: how Chinese newspapers framed the Coronavirus Disease 2019 (COVID-19) in its early stage. *Health, Risk & Society, 23*(3–4).

World Health Organization. (1981). *Global Strategy for Health for All by the Year 2000*. https://apps.who.int/iris/bitstream/handle/10665/38893/9241800038.pdf;jsessionid=0466F0DF59D3966A9F639C77A02ACB94?sequence=1

World Health Organization. (2020a). Q&A: how is COVID-19 transmitted? *World Health Organization*. www.who.int/emergencies/diseases/novel-coronavirus-2019/question-and-answers-hub/q-a-detail/q-a-how-is-covid-19-transmitted?gclid=CjwKCAjwsO_4BRBBEiwAyagRTTfHZ6hw7Q_pj5sMNnF8i5biRxj4b3polusXYBPGsmVNim03RwLbNxoC8R8QAvD_BwE

World Health Organization. (2020b). Timeline: WHO's COVID-19 response. www.who.int/emergencies/diseases/novel-coronavirus-2019/interactive-timeline?gclid=CjwKCAiA17P9BRB2EiwAMvwNyGWSa7LCiCAgb9r1TIgGmjmcYnZzOj7_zVA80ZeeVZyUsfqM35BvrhoCofQQAvD_BwE#event-7

World Health Organization. (2021a). Middle East respiratory syndrome coronavirus (MERS-CoV2). www.who.int/health-topics/middle-east-respiratory-syndrome-coronavirus-mers#tab=tab_1

World Health Organization. (2021b). Number of deaths due to HIV/AIDS. *World Health Organization*. www.who.int/data/gho/data/indicators/indicator-details/GHO/number-of-deaths-due-to-hiv-aids

World Health Organization. (2021c). WHO-convened global study of origins of SARS-CoV-2: China part. www.who.int/publications/i/item/who-convened-global-study-of-origins-of-sars-cov-2-china-part

Young, V. B. (2017). The role of the microbiome in human health and disease: an introduction for clinicians. *British Medical Journal, 356*. www.bmj.com/content/356/bmj.j831

2
THE MACROPOLITICS OF COVID
A political economy perspective

Introduction

In June 2021, the Chief Medical Officer of England, Professor Chris Whitty, gave a speech to a National Health Service conference in which he pointed the almost Dickensian nature of the distribution and socioeconomic effects of COVID in that country. Giving the example of the cities of Bradford and Leicester as well as underprivileged parts of London, he noted that these places

> have been hit over and over again in areas of deprivation. Indeed in many of them, if you had a map of COVID's biggest effects now and a map of child deaths in 1850, they look remarkably similar. These are areas where deprivation has been prolonged and deeply entrenched.
>
> itv.com, 2021

As Whitty's remarks suggest, the pattern of COVID infections and deaths in many countries and world regions display a close association with already existing socioeconomic disadvantage and marginalisation. Some commentators have consequently argued that the COVID pandemic has surfaced a 'crisis of care', in which the failings of neoliberal political and privatised approaches to public health surveillance systems and healthcare delivery across the world have been vividly revealed (The Care Collective, 2020).

This chapter uses the lens of Marxist-based critique, often referred to as the political economy perspective, to highlight the social determinants of health and healthcare. These critiques show how neoliberal and free market capitalist political systems have been called to account and disrupted by the COVID crisis but have also operated to protect the privileged. The political economy perspective incorporates discussion of macropolitical issues such as social justice, socioeconomic inequalities and the exacerbation of socioeconomic disadvantage caused by the pandemic, including the disproportionate effects on low-income countries and populations. Many questions are raised in these critiques about what the futures of neoliberal and capitalist systems may be in societies once the COVID crisis has subsided. In what follows, I provide an overview of the background of political economy analyses that refer to medicine and public health, including the concepts of capitalism, neoliberalism, medical dominance, the social determinants of health and globalisation. I then show how these concepts may be applied to an analysis of the macrostructural dimensions of the COVID crisis.

The political economy perspective

The political economy perspective applied to health and medical issues emerged in the 1970s, building on Marxian scholarship that discussed the role of capitalist economic systems and associated social structures and institutions such as government, the law, the education system and medicine in maintaining and reproducing social inequalities. German philosopher Karl Marx's revolutionary historical materialism thesis, formulated with Frederick Engels in response to the massive social, economic and political upheavals of the Industrial Revolution in nineteenth-century Europe, focused on the modes and relations of production and of exchange that were part of the economic systems of that era. Marx and Engels posited a direct critique of what they viewed as overly idealist and abstract German philosophy. They wanted to bring philosophical inquiry into the realities of everyday lives by addressing the generation of economic capital and how this operated as part of a social class–based system.

In writings such as The German Ideology, written in 1845–1846, Marx and Engels (2004) drew attention to the conditions under which the owners of the means of production (the industrialists or the bourgeoisie class) harnessed and profited from the physical work contributed by the labourers (or the proletariat class) in their factories, coal mines and mills. They argued that these industrialists owed their wealth to exploiting the bodily capacities of the workers, demanding backbreaking and often dangerous effort and long working hours from them in exchange for pay that barely kept them and their families alive. This was a materialist approach because it centred attention on the embodiment of workers' labour and their living and working conditions. Material realities governed social and political life and created people's consciousness of the world and their role in it.

For Marx and Engels, therefore, the key to improving the lives of the working class was to change the material conditions in which they lived and worked. They argued that people possessed some degree of agency, but this was limited by the conditions in which they found themselves. Power was conceptualised as an economic resource that was mostly owned and controlled by the ruling classes and state agencies and institutions, who used their power to maintain their wealth and authority by profiting from the labour of the working classes. At its most radical, exponents of Marxist philosophy call for the working class to rise up and engage in protests against their exploitation and for a new communist economic system that is governed by the state, where all citizens are treated equally. A less radical approach, as espoused in political economic analyses by sociologists and anthropologists, operates to highlight the macropolitical dimensions of the social injustices and inequalities that continue to exist worldwide.

From the late 1970s, neoliberalism, a new ideological approach to political governance, has provided a major target for political economy critiques. Beginning with the policies instituted by President Ronald Reagan and Prime Minister Margaret Thatcher in the USA and UK, respectively, and spreading to many other countries around the world since then, the neoliberalist political philosophy positions the market as dominant in shaping how social and economic systems operate. The concept of the 'small state' is a major part of neoliberalism, involving low levels of direct intervention by governments into the capitalist economic system but enough of a role to ensure its effective functioning (defined as promoting economic wealth and security for nation states). Neoliberalist policies therefore support social groups and social institutions who benefit from the wealth generated by capitalism and minimise state support for the socioeconomically disadvantaged. These policies promote an individualistic approach to access to life opportunities, positioning people as ideally taking responsibility to better themselves or protect their interests. The neoliberal ethos therefore works to lessen citizens' reliance on social welfare and other forms of state support. As critics have pointed out, this ideology furthers the interests of the powerful and the wealthy while adopting a punitive and uncaring approach to the most underprivileged social groups (Roberts, 2020; Schrecker, 2016).

Feminist critiques have built on political economy perspectives by introducing a gender lens on structural inequality, emphasising that previous Marxian analyses have often ignored the intersections of social class with gender. Emerging and expanding with the second wave feminist movement in the 1970s, what is now a vast literature of feminist research has demonstrated the continuing entrenched sexism that limits the life opportunities for women, positioning them as inferior to men and excluding them from achieving power and status (Smith, 1989). The critical disability studies literature offers a further application of political economy perspectives by emphasising the ways that capitalist and neoliberal political ideologies and practices work to marginalise disabled people and restrict their life opportunities. This literature focuses particularly on institutions such as the education, employment and healthcare systems and how these institutions perpetuate the marginalisation of disabled people by positioning them as inferior to other people, challenging the 'ableism' that excludes disabled people from full participation in society (Goodley et al., 2017).

Other extensions of critical perspectives building on political economy theory are critical race theory and postcolonial theory. Critical race theory and the postcolonialism perspective both devote attention to the persistent racism, racialisation and Othering that is evident in the legacy of colonial histories (King, 2002; Treviño et al., 2008). Building on Marxist theory, critical race theorists turn their attention to how institutions such as the policing and justice system perpetuate racism and limit the life opportunities of racial minorities. They pay particular attention to colourism: discrimination against people based on their skin colour in sociocultural contexts in which whiteness is privileged (Treviño et al., 2008). Postcolonial perspectives identify the structural causes of racism and the sociocultural and political legacy left by colonialism and imperialism practices. They draw attention to the structural social inequalities and racist ideologies that led to colonialists invading countries and subjugating, exploiting and often murdering the peoples already occupying the land. They also address the consequences of decolonisation of countries once colonialists have left or given up authority over the original inhabitants (Bhambra, 2014).

Political economy perspectives on medicine and public health

The institution of scientific medicine in capitalist economies and those who practised it have often been positioned in political economy critiques as focusing on maintaining authority and power rather than working to alleviate the health effects caused by social inequalities. Landmark publications appearing during the 1970s, such as the US sociologists Eliot Freidson's (1970) book *Professional Dominance* and Vicente Navarro's (1976) *Medicine Under Capitalism* as well as British sociologists Lesley Doyal and Imogen Pennell's (1979) book *The Political Economy of Health*, were influential in challenging the status quo. Particularly from the perspective of medical sociologists and anthropologists adopting a political economy lens in the USA, where healthcare has been largely privatised and run as a corporate enterprise, medical practitioners are viewed as privileged and highly paid professionals who have continually sought to maintain their status as the primary experts on diagnosis and medical care. In national contexts in which healthcare is largely or solely offered as a government-funded service to all citizens, such as the UK, Australia and parts of Europe, the political economy critique offers a somewhat different approach. Social researchers commenting on these medical systems have identified the role of government in maintaining medical authority and dominance together with the influence wrought by the medical profession.

In more recent times, writers adopting the political economy perspective have emphasised the role of socioeconomic factor in structuring different social groups' experiences of health and illness. These critics have pointed out entrenched differences in patterns of disease, death rates and life expectancy between those who are privileged compared with those who struggle with less favourable circumstances. The term 'social determinants of health' is often used to describe these factors (Marmot & Wilkinson, 2005). Many studies have demonstrated that sociodemographic factors such as low income, poverty, employment in dangerous occupations, living in poor housing conditions or regions with high levels of air pollution, or dealing with exclusion from opportunities or support because of disability, racism, sexism or homophobia contribute to comparatively worse health status and greater death rates. Critics have also observed how socioeconomically advantaged people's access to high-quality healthcare in capitalist systems of medicine is much greater than less-advantaged social groups (Goodley et al., 2017; Harvey, 2020; Marmot & Wilkinson, 2005; Sell & Williams, 2020). Political economy critiques have also drawn attention to capitalist system's support of 'Big Pharma': the major global pharmaceutical companies that wield enormous power and reap massive profits from their products (Harvey, 2020; Sell & Williams, 2020).

Medical anthropologists adopting a political economy approach have shown how healthcare systems in low-income countries are often underfunded, with continuing poor access to pharmaceuticals, vaccines and healthcare professionals. Improvements in public health interventions which are taken for granted by people in high-income countries, such as sanitation, food security and access to clean drinking water, remain major causes of illness, disease and high mortality rates compared with the Global North (Singer & Baer, 2018). Postcolonial ideologies are often a major contributor to exploiting colonised populations in ways that detract from their health, including continued social marginalisation and exclusion, entrenched poverty and racism. In wealthy postcolonial countries such as Australia, New Zealand, the USA and Canada, for example, there are major disparities in the health status and life expectancy of Indigenous compared with settler populations (Paradies, 2016).

Anthropologist Merrill Singer's (2009) concept of the syndemic (discussed in the Introduction chapter) is a political economy approach to pandemics. He describes the concept as a critical systems theory approach to community and public health, including political and economic structures together with biological, cultural and spatial dimensions of disease. Singer first developed this approach in his research on health disparities and the HIV/AIDS epidemic, primarily working in a Latino and African-American inner-city neighbourhood in the USA. He noticed how socioeconomic disadvantage and racism intertwined with greater susceptibility to illness and disease. Singer drew attention to the importance of relieving the burden of disease in disadvantaged communities through improving their income, living conditions and access to education and healthcare. As Singer points out, it is only until these broader socioeconomic causes of disadvantage and marginalisation are addressed that syndemics such as HIV/AIDS, with its co-occurring diseases such as hepatitis B, malnutrition and tuberculosis, together with practices such as injecting drug use, can be alleviated.

As neoliberalism ideologies began to be taken up by governments across the globe, an approach to healthcare and health promotion began to emerge which focused on citizens' responsibility for protecting and preserving their good health and avoiding activities such as smoking, over-consumption of alcohol, injecting drug use and eating a poor diet (Schrecker, 2016). People were expected to become 'empowered' to take control of their health: including seeking out information, taking notice of public health campaigns about avoiding risky practices and acting on these messages of self-discipline (Lupton, 1995). Meanwhile, the social determinants of ill-health, disease and premature mortality tended to be ignored or unaddressed, as they required government's attention to improving underlying social structural factors such as poverty and poor housing (Goodley et al., 2017; Marmot & Wilkinson, 2005). These tensions have become even more intense in the period following the global financial crisis of 2008, in which many governments instituted austerity measures, including reducing expenditure on social welfare even further. These measures have in turn widened the gaps between the living conditions, income, health status and life expectancy experienced by the wealthy and the poor (Schrecker, 2016).

Social commentators adopting a political economy perspective have frequently commented on social changes wrought by macrostructural forces such as globalisation and how they have contributed to health inequalities. Globalisation refers to the expansion of forms of economic infrastructures, consumption, communication networks and political governance from specific locations to across the world, as well as increased mobilities of people internationally (Huynen et al., 2005). Globalisation has both beneficial and harmful effects on human health. It has stabilised some economies and led to some nations improving their economic standing, and in turn, alleviating poverty and building better healthcare systems. New medical and public health knowledge and alerts can now be more easily shared across regions. National disease surveillance systems can readily communicate with each other. However, some populations remain mired in poverty, including previously colonised populations living in settler societies, while increasing economic production has contributed to environmental pollution, climate change and global warming (Huynen et al., 2005).

In the case of communicable diseases, the expansion of intensive farming, deforestation, the destruction of wildlife habitats and the expansion in mass international travel have all contributed to new disease outbreaks. Air travel has increased fourfold since 1990, with the consequence that a pathogen can spread around the world very quickly (The Independent Panel for Pandemic Preparedness & Response, 2021). Most of the new pathogens emerging over the past half-century are zoonotic in origin. Factors such as extensive forest clearing, urban development, increasing demands for food security and associated changes in large-scale agriculture have facilitated the destruction of wildlife's natural habits and increased wild animals' contact with humans and domestic or farmed animals, contributing to opportunities for viruses to move from animals to humans (The Independent Panel for Pandemic Preparedness & Response, 2021).

Globalisation has also contributed to what has been described as 'global health' approaches, which themselves are often intensely political. Global health has become part of international relations and diplomacy. International approaches to healthcare delivery and public health efforts are underpinned by political relationships and networks. The pharmaceutical industry is now global. Peak bodies such as WHO, the World Trade Organization and the World Bank seek to manage and coordinate health prevention efforts across the world, together with national governments, community and activist organisations, charitable foundations and for-profit enterprises. However, preparations for new disease outbreaks in high-income countries have often tended to ignore the broader socioeconomic conditions that contribute to these outbreaks, in favour of technical responses and pharmaceutical development (Davies et al., 2014; Ruckert et al., 2016).

The political economy of COVID-19

The national political forms of government, social institutions and ideologies existing before the emergence of SARS-CoV-2 were a major influence on how well or badly the outbreak was managed over its first year. Neoliberal political systems could no longer rely on the free market to solve the broad and deep problems associated with the pandemic. The citizens of countries with populist libertarian or authoritarian leaders and governments, including Brazil, India, the USA and the UK, suffered from extremely poor control of the pandemic due to the inadequate responses – or in some cases, simple lack of action by their governments. Early in the pandemic, it appeared that capitalism was failing, as prominently exemplified by the USA, the richest country globally, leading the world in numbers of COVID cases and deaths due to poor prevention strategies and indeed outright neglect on the part of the federal government under the Trump administration.

Throughout 2020, former President Donald Trump's last year in office, he continued the domineering form of masculine leadership that marked his four-year term (Thomson, 2020). Trump refused to acknowledge the severity of the health risks posed by COVID to Americans: particularly those who were socioeconomically disadvantaged. He continually prioritised the economy and protected the interests of the wealthy over the health and well-being of these social groups. Trump repeatedly claimed that he was controlling the spread of COVID effectively. He deliberately undermined, contradicted or suppressed authorities such as the Centers for Disease Control and Dr Anthony Fauci, a foremost infectious disease expert in the USA and Director of the National Institute of Allergy and Infectious Diseases. Trump also withdrew the US government's support for WHO and made continual public statements challenging the idea that wearing masks was an effective measure to protect people against infection. Even when Trump himself became infected with COVID, he avoided wearing a mask in public and derided his political opponent (and now President) Joe Biden for doing so (Lupton et al., 2021).

UK's government, led by Prime Minister Boris Johnson, was also more laissez faire in its approach to COVID containment compared with many other governments. Early on the pandemic, Johnson was loath to impose restrictions on UK citizens or close international borders. His strategy was first to aim for 'natural' herd immunity by letting the novel coronavirus spread unchecked (Scambler, 2020). Johnson continued with this policy even after it was clear that lack of restrictions would lead to far greater problems: first from the experiences of European countries such as Italy and Spain that were among the first to be devastated by exponential rises in COVID cases and deaths, and then from the massive increase in cases and deaths in the UK itself. A notion of the cultural superiority of the British, including the country's championing of the ideals of freedom and liberty and a desire to avoid interventionist 'big government' measures, led to the government's refusal to adopt strategies such as closing of businesses and restaurants and a national lockdown as early as some other countries did (Meghji & Niang, 2021).

The Swedish government's Public Health Agency also became renowned globally for its libertarian approach to COVID containment policy in the early stages of the pandemic. It also seemed to be aiming for herd immunity by letting infections spread rampantly and avoiding mandated strategies such as physical distancing, stay-at-home orders, banning large group activities and face masking in public. By the end of 2020, the consequences were starkly apparent. Sweden had recorded COVID deaths at a per capita rate that was 4.5–10 times those of its Nordic neighbours, despite similar health systems and socioeconomic profiles (Claeson & Hanson, 2021).

Some governments that had traditionally relied on neoliberal 'small state' policies were forced to relax their political ideologies as they hastened to deal with the catastrophic economic conditions induced by COVID control measures. They introduced severely restrictive state-led measures such as closing international borders, limiting air travel, cancelling immigration programmes, forcing business shutdowns, closing schools and requiring work-from-home restrictions as part of lockdowns: all of which had detrimental knock-on effects on the economy. Despite otherwise unhelpful approaches, the federal and state governments during the Trump administration tried to forestall the collapse of the US economy by adopting stimulus packages worth trillions of dollars that improved social welfare provisions (Roberts, 2020). When new US President Joe Biden replaced Trump in early 2021, he immediately directed funds to providing mass vaccination programmes, continued to advocate for mask wearing as a preventive agent against COVID infections and approved further public spending programmes. The neoliberalist ethos of the US government had shifted dramatically at the same time as the havoc wrought by the austerity cost-cutting of the previous two decades was becoming painfully apparent, as evidenced by the healthcare system struggling to treat COVID patients during the surges in demand as cases quickly increased in number throughout 2020 (Roberts, 2020).

Similar responses were evident in other governments that had previously adhered closely to the principles of neoliberalism in economic management. Such governments, including Germany, Australia, New Zealand, Austria, France, Sweden – and eventually, the UK – were forced to provide generous economic support not only to business but also to individuals who had lost their income due to lockdown measures, so as to prevent a breakdown in their capitalist systems (Altiparmakis et al., 2021). Australia and New Zealand, both island nations with relatively small populations, adopted a 'COVID elimination' approach that relied on closing their international borders early on the pandemic, instituting a mandatory period of strict quarantine on all incoming travellers and imposing severe controls on the number of expatriate citizens who could return. It became very difficult for people to leave or enter either country, with exemptions offered for a limited range of reasons. These strategies rewarded Australia and New Zealand with excellent control of case numbers and deaths and few extended lockdown periods in the first year of the pandemic. However, these strategies caused major economic impacts and widespread job losses for industries such as travel, hospitality and tourism that relied on international visitors, requiring significant compensation from the government.

Social research has demonstrated that political and religious beliefs can play a strong role in people's willingness to engage in preventive actions against the spread of COVID. People who hold more conservative views are more likely to eschew measures such as face mask wearing and accepting vaccination compared with those aligned on the progressive side of politics because of holding libertarian ideologies that resist the idea of 'big government'. For example, surveys of the US population by the Pew Research Center found that while approximately seven out of ten Americans said that they probably or definitely would get vaccinated in February 2021 (including 19% who had already had at least one dose), people who voted towards the left (83%) were more likely to get vaccinated compared with those who are more politically conservative (56%). White evangelical Christians (just over 50%) were far less likely than atheists (90%) to be positive about being inoculated against COVID or reporting having already received a dose. Political conservatives have also continually contended that COVID is not a major public health risk (Funk & Gramlich, 2021).

In the early stages of the pandemic, some prominent economists began to assert that the crisis could disrupt the capitalist economic system by exposing its flaws, leading to a rebuilding of economies in more sustainable and inclusive ways (Stevano et al., 2021). However, as the COVID crisis has continued and worsened, it has become clear that as a form of 'disaster capitalism' (Klein, 2020), the capitalist economic system has continued to exploit the working class and profit from state funding. Disaster capitalism involves neoliberal and capitalist systems of government working together to fund private companies, including for-profit transnational corporations, to provide support to the victims of catastrophes (Klein, 2020). Governments use state funding in these endeavours, from which private companies are able to profit, rather than directly providing social welfare to their citizens (Schuller & Maldonado, 2016). Examples of such arrangements since the emergence of the COVID crisis have included the governor of New York City, Andrew Cuomo, entering into partnerships with the Bill and Melinda Gates Foundation and Google involving the introduction of 'smart' technologies to support endeavours such as telehealth provision and working and learning from home for the city's residents (Klein, 2020). Some critics have characterised these arrangements as 'less symbiotic than parasitic', with profit motives triumphing over effective and inclusive support (Mazzucato, 2020).

Meanwhile, many individuals and companies who were already extremely wealthy have benefited financially from the COVID crisis. Two examples are Amazon and Walmart, both of whom reported billions of additional profits during the first year of the pandemic, largely due to the massive increase in online shopping that resulted from lockdowns and restrictions of people's movements imposed by governments. Their low-paid frontline workers received very little increase in their pay, while shareholders in the companies were handsomely rewarded. The fortune of Jeff Bezos, Amazon founder and already the wealthiest person in the world, increased by US$75.6 billion between March and December 2020 (Kinder & Stateler, 2020). Major global pharmaceutical companies who are developing and manufacturing COVID vaccines, including Moderna and Pfizer, also expect soaring profits as the vaccines are rolled out globally (Kollewe, 2021).

Another example of the continuing power of global organisations was evident in Japan's struggles in hosting the 2021 Summer Olympic and Paralympic Games in Tokyo resulting from disputes and tensions fuelled by the power wielded by the International Olympics Committee (IOC). The Games were due to be held in 2020 but were delayed until 2021 because of the pandemic. Despite growing numbers of COVID infections in Japan, a state of emergency declared for Tokyo, low national vaccination rates and general opposition to the Olympics on the part of the Japanese public and medical and public health experts in the weeks leading up to the postponed date of the Olympics, the Games still went ahead, albeit with restrictions imposed such as a ban on spectators. The decision to press on with holding the Games was driven by economic and political constraints. For the Japanese government and Prime Minister Yoshihide Suga, facing an election, holding the Games was a matter of international prestige as well as a promise of improving the country's economy through increased tourism. Further, due to contractual constraints imposed by legal agreements with the IOC, the government could not easily cancel the Games. Voicing platitudes about the Games' capacity to provide a 'light at the end of the tunnel' and intimations of a 'post-corona world', members of the IOC and their supporters forced the Japanese government's hand in ensuring that the Games went ahead in apparent flagrant denial of the risks they were imposing not only to Japanese citizens but also to the attending international athletes and officials and the populations of their countries (Jefferson Lenskyj, 2021).

Social inequalities and the COVID syndemic

Long-standing socioeconomic inequities and inefficiencies associated with neoliberal forms of governance and the austerity measures that had been introduced following the global financial crisis were not only exposed but also exacerbated by the outbreak as it increased with exponential speed around the world. The Independent Panel for Pandemic Preparedness & Response's (2021) report on the global response to the COVID crisis listed the many economic effects of the crisis and the major impacts on sustainable development. These effects include the loss of an estimated US$10 trillion of output by the end of 2021 and US$22 trillion between 2020 and 2025: predicted to be the deepest shock to the global economy since World War II. The Panel's report further detailed that across the world, those people who were already in socioeconomically disadvantaged situations before the emergence of the pandemic, including migrants, refugees and displaced people, have experienced the worst effects on their health, living standards and income. At the time the report was published, it was estimated that between 115 and 125 million people had already been pushed into extreme poverty by the continuing crisis.

Many low- and middle-income countries in the Global South first appeared to have handled the COVID crisis well compared with the UK, Spain, Italy, France and USA: countries where COVID spread quickly during the early months of the pandemic. With the emergence of the more infectious Delta variant in the early months of 2021, however, several countries began to experience significant increases in COVID cases and deaths. India's COVID cases seemed relatively low during 2020, despite major social problems when a sudden lockdown was imposed, and thousands of the country's lowest paid workers fled from the major cities to their native villages. By May 2021, the situation had dramatically worsened. Driven by the Delta variant and the lifting of restrictions leading to large gatherings such as political rallies and religious festivals involving millions of people, India's COVID cases and deaths had begun to rise rapidly, breaking previous global records for daily numbers even as many experts suggested that the real figures were under-reported (The New York Times, 2021).

In numerous low-income countries, including India, Myanmar, Afghanistan, Indonesia, Sudan and Zimbabwe, adequate financial support or other forms of social welfare have not been provided for people who have been forced into lockdown or lost employment in other ways due to COVID. In a context in which already fragile health systems have been overwhelmed, many people have considered the risk of contracting COVID as far lower than the more imminent danger of starvation or perishing from other conditions such as HIV/AIDS, tuberculosis or malaria (Ruppel et al., 2021). As Ruppel and colleagues (2021) point out:

> In the absence of accessible healthcare for the poor, the coronavirus can be expected to spread freely: if you have no home, you cannot go home during a lockdown; if you have no clean water, you cannot follow hygiene measures; if you live as a whole family in one room with neighbours next door under the same conditions, social distancing is simply not possible.

Even within wealthy countries, major disparities exist between socioeconomically advantaged and disadvantaged groups in terms of how many have become seriously ill or died from COVID. In the USA, people who had university-level education and were able to work from home fared far better in the COVID crisis than did others. One in five Americans reported that the pandemic had negatively affected their job or career or those of people they know. Educators, healthcare workers and those in other essential jobs were particularly likely to encounter difficulties in their jobs. Only 13% mentioned improvements in their working situation, but these people tended to be those who could easily work from home and had ready access to digital technologies to support their work. University-educated people were more than twice as likely as those with a lower level of education (21% compared with 8%) to say that their work situation had improved, and those with higher incomes also reported more positive work experiences. More than one in five Americans mentioned that they or others they knew had experienced economic difficulties during the crisis, resulting from job loss (van Kessel et al., 2021).

A critical race theory combined with a postcolonial approach to how people of colour were treated in the UK during the first wave of COVID has highlighted the role of racism and racialisation in the significant exacerbation of their disadvantage during this period. British people of colour were more likely to lose their source of income than white Britons during the lockdown because they worked in industries that were closed and had less savings to cover periods of unemployment. Statistics from the UK also demonstrate the disproportionate impact of COVID on Black, Asian and minority ethnic communities. The first ten healthcare professionals to die from COVID in the UK were from these communities. Data from April 2020 showed that one-third of patients admitted to critical care units were from an ethnic minority group. The post-racial rationalising of the disproportionate number of deaths from COVID of people of colour meant that state institutions tended to deny that structural racism was the underlying cause of these deaths and socioeconomic disadvantage. These kinds of explanations lead to a victim-blaming discourse in which it is argued that people of colour need to help themselves by breaking free of the constraints of historical racism or of their cultural and 'lifestyle' practices rather than recognising the structural forms of disadvantage in which they are living (Meghji & Niang, 2021).

In the USA, Black and Latino populations experienced a disproportionate number of illness and deaths from COVID, reversing over ten years of progress in closing the Black–White gap in life expectancy. In February 2021, a survey of US adults found that Black Americans were notably more concerned than other racial/ethnic groups about their personal risk of contracting COVID and in viewing the pandemic as a serious public health threat. This survey also found that almost 80% of Black American adults personally knew someone who has been hospitalised or died from COVID. This finding is not surprising in the light of data showing that Black life expectancy has fallen by 2.7 years from pre-COVID levels, compared with only one year for the American population as a whole (Johnson & Funk, 2021).

Whereas Latinos had better life expectancies than white Americans prior to COVID, it has been estimated that this advantage was reduced by over 70% in the wake of the pandemic's effects in that country (Andrasfay & Goldman, 2021).

The reasons for these greater numbers can be attributed to a combination of higher socioeconomic disadvantage and social stress experienced by people of colour in the USA and UK, cultural differences in living arrangements (such as number of people in households), a greater likelihood of pre-existing health conditions that can exacerbate the effects of coronavirus infection and the higher participation of people of colour in occupations that involve person-to-person interactions, thereby exposing them to heightened risk of contracting infection (Phiri et al., 2021). These conditions reveal the syndemic that combines racism, poor or crowded housing conditions, co-morbidities, low income and poverty with higher-risk working conditions in generating greater risk for people of colour in high-income countries.

Existing socioeconomic inequalities based on gender and sexuality have also intensified throughout the world. Social and economic analyses have demonstrated that hard-won progress towards gender equality globally has been forestalled or wound back since the advent of COVID. Long-standing gender inequalities in the division of household and paid labour together with assumptions about women's primary role in caring for children and older relatives have traditionally limited women's opportunities to participate fully in the paid workforce. Not surprisingly, therefore, during the COVID crisis, women in many countries across the world have borne the brunt of family caregiving as they attempt to combine their paid work with supervising children who are learning from home and the care of other family members. Consequently, women have had to limit their participation in paid work more than have men (FP Analytics, 2021; Madgavkar et al., 2020).

Pre-COVID, women across the Global South were already suffering from lower participation in and access to the paid workforce compared with men, due to sexism and other cultural barriers. Women and girls were also often denied equal opportunities to access digital technologies. Once stay-at-home orders were implemented and schools closed during lockdowns, many women and girls were faced with not being able to work or learn from home because they were denied the opportunity to engage online (Madgavkar et al.,

2020). Women were already disproportionately represented in industries that declined the most during the pandemic, such as the informal economy, hospitality and food services and retail (FP Analytics, 2021; Madgavkar et al., 2020). A global survey across 40 countries found that 55% of the surveyed women cited income loss as the greatest impact of COVID on their lives, compared to 34% of male respondents. It has been estimated that the pandemic could force up to 20 million secondary school girls in low- and middle-income countries to leave school permanently as they are required to take up unpaid care work (FP Analytics, 2021).

Further, as more women than men tend to be employed in paid frontline care work involving close proximity to other people, such as nursing, hospital aids and assistants, childcare and carers for older people, they have been exposed to greater risk of COVID infection (Yarrow & Pagan, 2020). The incidence of partner-led violence against women has increased dramatically in many parts of the world during periods of stay-at-home restrictions (FP Analytics, 2021; Stevano et al., 2021). The home can also be an unsafe place for LGBTQI people who live in shared accommodation or with homophobic family members. Places such as clubs and bars where queer people were able to safely meet have in many cases shut down permanently due to loss of revenue during COVID-related shutdowns and lockdowns (Trott, 2020).

Researchers from critical disability studies have argued that disabled people face a 'triple jeopardy' in COVID societies. They are differentially affected by the pandemic because of three factors: first, the increased risk of poor outcomes from COVID if they become infected; second, reduced access to routine healthcare and rehabilitation; and third, the adverse social and economic effects of restrictions introduced to mitigate the spread of SARS-CoV-2 (Shakespeare et al., 2021). In some countries, people with disabilities have been far more vulnerable to infection, illness and death from COVID compared with other social groups, often exacerbated by already existing inequalities such as living in poverty, mobility difficulties and isolation from the community, including less access to digital technologies to support online work and socialising (Banks et al., 2021). Disabled people often live in group housing or residential homes: places that have been sources of rampant novel coronavirus spread due to difficulties in containing infection. These impacts from the pandemic are simply the latest examples of lack of preparation and support for people with disabilities during emergencies and crises even in high-income countries (Shakespeare et al., 2021).

Building on Singer's work and others using the syndemic approach, the synergistic interactions of COVID with social inequality and chronic disease (Islam et al., 2021), HIV and food insecurity (McLinden et al., 2020), injecting drug use, overdose, HIV and hepatitis C (Bonn et al., 2020), environmental health (Kenyon, 2020) and non-communicable diseases such as diabetes, hypertension, cardiovascular disease and chronic lung disease (Yadav et al., 2020) have been noted by epidemiologists and community health researchers across the world. One particularly confronting example of a COVID-related syndemic is the rapid spread of a fungal disease, mucormycosis, during the second COVID wave in India in mid-2021. If established in the human body, this fungal infection invades the tissues of the face, jaw and brain, blocking blood flow and causing the skin and organs to die, resulting in discoloured tissue that led the Indian news media to use the colloquial term 'black fungus' to describe the disease. The fungi are widespread and usually are easily dealt with by the body, but in situations where people's immune systems are weakened or compromised, or if they already have poorly controlled diabetes, the infection is more likely to take hold. Mucormycosis is also linked to the use of therapeutic steroids, which some Indian healthcare institutions have been employing in a desperate attempt to treat the large numbers of severely ill COVID cases with whom they were dealing during the second wave. The steroids help patients who need supplemental oxygen but also lead to weakened immune systems. In this devastating situation, an existing disease (diabetes) had come together with COVID in a healthcare context in which necessary treatments to control both diseases were not available, thereby leading to a greater burden of disease and death (Schwartz & Chakrabati, 2021).

Concluding comments

The political economy perspective demonstrates that prolonged crises such as the COVID pandemic can have major impacts on structural elements of social relations, organisations and governance. In the face of the multitude of health, social and economic threats posed by the COVID outbreak, the unifying concept of global health has broken down. On the one hand, the rapid spread of the novel coronavirus around the world is evidence of the major elements of globalisation. On the other hand, however, nationalism and regionalism have emerged as stronger than ever, as nation states and even regions within nations have competed to protect their citizens and achieve political support by imposing restrictions on entry of people from outside their borders. The crisis has exposed not only the entrenched structural inequalities that persist in every country around the world, but also the deficiencies of neoliberal and 'small government' approaches that rely on citizens to shoulder the responsibility for protecting themselves from disease and the socioeconomic harms of the COVID crisis. Chapter 3 will examine these issues from a Foucauldian perspective, devoting greater attention to how macropolitical and micropolitical dimensions intertwine as citizens, state authorities and social institutions struggle to make sense of and contain the crisis.

References

Altiparmakis, A., Bojar, A., Brouard, S., Foucault, M., Kriesi, H., & Nadeau, R. (2021). Pandemic politics: policy evaluations of government responses to COVID-19. *West European Politics*, *44*(5–6), 1159–1179.

Andrasfay, T., & Goldman, N. (2021). Reductions in 2020 US life expectancy due to COVID-19 and the disproportionate impact on the Black and Latino populations. *Proceedings of the National Academy of Sciences*, *118*(5). www.pnas.org/content/118/5/e2014746118.abstract

Banks, L. M., Davey, C., Shakespeare, T., & Kuper, H. (2021). Disability-inclusive responses to COVID-19: lessons learnt from research on social protection in low-and middle-income countries. *World Development*, *137*. https://doi.org/10.1016/j.worlddev.2020.105178

Bhambra, G. K. (2014). Postcolonial and decolonial dialogues. *Postcolonial Studies*, *17*(2), 115–121.

Bonn, M., Palayew, A., Bartlett, S., Brothers, T. D., Touesnard, N., & Tyndall, M. (2020). Addressing the syndemic of HIV, hepatitis C, overdose, and COVID-19 among people who use drugs: the potential roles for decriminalization and safe supply. *Journal of Studies on Alcohol and Drugs*, *81*(5), 556–560.

Claeson, M., & Hanson, S. (2021). COVID-19 and the Swedish enigma. *The Lancet*, *397*(10271), 259–261.

Davies, S. E., Elbe, S., Howell, A., & McInnes, C. (2014). Global health in international relations: editors' introduction. *Review of International Studies*, *40*(5), 825–834.

Doyal, L., & Pennell, I. (1979). *The Political Economy of Health*. Pluto Press.

FP Analytics. (2021). Elevating gender equality in COVID-19 economic recovery. *FP Analytics*. https://genderequalitycovid19recovery.com/

Freidson, E. (1970). *Professional Dominance: The Social Structure of Medical Care.* Transaction Publishers.
Funk, C., & Gramlich, J. (2021). 10 facts about Americans and coronavirus vaccines. *Pew Research Center.* www.pewresearch.org/fact-tank/2021/03/23/10-facts-about-americans-and-coronavirus-vaccines/
Goodley, D., Lawthom, R., Liddiard, K., & Cole, K. R. (2017). Critical disability studies. In B. Gough (Ed.), *The Palgrave Handbook of Critical Social Psychology* (pp. 491–505). Palgrave.
Harvey, M. (2020). The political economy of health: revisiting its Marxian origins to address 21st-century health inequalities. *American Journal of Public Health, 111*(2), 293–300.
Huynen, M. M., Martens, P., & Hilderink, H. B. (2005). The health impacts of globalisation: a conceptual framework. *Globalization and Health, 1*(1). https://globalizationandhealth.biomedcentral.com/articles/10.1186/1744-8603-1-14
Islam, N., Lacey, B., Shabnam, S., Erzurumluoglu, A. M., Dambha-Miller, H., Chowell, G., Kawachi, I., & Marmot, M. (2021). Social inequality and the syndemic of chronic disease and COVID-19: county-level analysis in the USA. *Journal of Epidemiology and Community Health, 75*(6), 496–500.
itv.com. (2021). Covid 'has not thrown its last surprise at us', warns Chris Whitty. www.itv.com/news/2021-06-17/covid-has-not-thrown-its-last-surprise-at-us-warns-chris-whitty
Jefferson Lenskyj, H. (2021). Holding the Tokyo Olympics without spectators during COVID-19 emergency puts the IOC's 'supreme authority' on full display. *The Conversation.* https://theconversation.com/holding-the-tokyo-olympics-without-spectators-during-covid-19-emergency-puts-the-iocs-supreme-authority-on-full-display-163702
Johnson, C., & Funk, C. (2021). Black Americans stand out for their concern about COVID-19; 61% say that they plan to get vaccinated or already have. *Pew Research Center.* www.pewresearch.org/fact-tank/2021/03/09/black-americans-stand-out-for-their-concern-about-covid-19-61-say-they-plan-to-get-vaccinated-or-already-have/
Kenyon, C. (2020). Syndemic responses to COVID-19 should include an ecological dimension. *The Lancet, 396*(10264), 1730–1731.
Kinder, M., & Stateler, L. (2020). Amazon and Walmart have raked in billions in additional profits during the pandemic, and shared almost none of it with their workers. *Brookings.* www.brookings.edu/blog/the-avenue/2020/12/22/amazon-and-walmart-have-raked-in-billions-in-additional-profits-during-the-pandemic-and-shared-almost-none-of-it-with-their-workers/
King, N. B. (2002). Security, disease, commerce: ideologies of postcolonial global health. *Social Studies of Science, 32*(5–6), 763–789.
Klein, N. (2020). Naomi Klein: how big tech plans to profit from the pandemic. *The Guardian.* www.theguardian.com/news/2020/may/13/naomi-klein-how-big-tech-plans-to-profit-from-coronavirus-pandemic

Kollewe, J. (2021). From Pfizer and Moderna: who's making billions from COVID-19 vaccines? *The Guardian*. www.theguardian.com/business/2021/mar/06/from-pfizer-to-moderna-whos-making-billions-from-covid-vaccines

Lupton, D. (1995). *The Imperative of Health: Public Health and the Regulated Body*. Sage.

Lupton, D., Southerton, C., Clark, M., & Watson, A. (2021). *The Face Mask in COVID Times: A Sociomaterial Analysis*. De Gruyter.

Madgavkar, A., White, O., Krishnan, M., Mahajan, D., & Azcue, X. (2020). *COVID-19 and Gender Equality: Countering the Regressive Effects*. McKinsey Global Institute. www.apucis.com/frontend-assets/porto/initial-reports/COVID-19-and-gender-equality-Countering-the-regressive-effects-vF.pdf.pagespeed.ce.DDg-UdcoaA.pdf

Marmot, M., & Wilkinson, R. (Eds.). (2005). *Social Determinants of Health* (2nd ed.). Oxford University Press.

Marx, K., & Engels, F. (2004). *The German Ideology*. International Publishers.

Mazzucato, M. (2020). Coronavirus and capitalism: How will the virus change the way the world works? *World Economic Forum*. www.weforum.org/agenda/2020/04/coronavirus-covid19-business-economics-society-economics-change

McLinden, T., Stover, S., & Hogg, R. S. (2020). HIV and food insecurity: a syndemic amid the COVID-19 pandemic. *AIDS and Behavior*, 24, 2766–2769.

Meghji, A., & Niang, S. M. (2021). Between post-racial ideology and provincial universalisms: critical race theory, decolonial thought and COVID-19 in Britain. *Sociology*, online first. https://doi.org/10.1177/00380385211011575

Navarro, V. (1976). *Medicine under Capitalism*. Prodist.

Paradies, Y. (2016). Colonisation, racism and indigenous health. *Journal of Population Research*, 33(1), 83–96.

Phiri, P., Delanerolle, G., Al-Sudani, A., & Rathod, S. (2021). COVID-19 and Black, Asian, and minority ethnic communities: a complex relationship without just cause. *JMIR Public Health Surveillance*, 7(2). https://publichealth.jmir.org/2021/2/e22581

Roberts, A. (2020). The third and fatal shock: how pandemic killed the millennial paradigm. *Public Administration Review*, 80(4), 603–609.

Ruckert, A., Labonté, R., Lencucha, R., Runnels, V., & Gagnon, M. (2016). Global health diplomacy: a critical review of the literature. *Social Science & Medicine*, 155, 61–72.

Ruppel, A., Halim, M. I., Kikon, R., Mohamed, N. S., & Saebipour, M. R. (2021). Could COVID-19 be contained in poor populations by herd immunity rather than by strategies designed for affluent societies or potential vaccine(s)? *Global Health Action*, 14(1). https://doi.org/10.1080/16549716.2020.1863129

Scambler, G. (2020). Covid-19 as a 'breaching experiment': exposing the fractured society. *Health Sociology Review*, 29(2), 140–148.

Schrecker, T. (2016). Neoliberalism and health: the linkages and the dangers. *Sociology Compass*, *10*(10), 952–971.
Schuller, M., & Maldonado, J. K. (2016). Disaster capitalism. *Annals of Anthropological Practice*, *40*(1), 61–72.
Schwartz, I., & Chakrabati, A. (2021). 'Black fungus' is creating a whole other health emergency for COVID-stricken India. *The Guardian*. www.theguardian.com/commentisfree/2021/jun/02/black-fungus-covid-india-mucormycosis
Sell, S. K., & Williams, O. D. (2020). Health under capitalism: a global political economy of structural pathogenesis. *Review of International Political Economy*, *27*(1), 1–25.
Shakespeare, T., Ndagire, F., & Seketi, Q. E. (2021). Triple jeopardy: disabled people and the COVID-19 pandemic. *The Lancet*, *397*(10282). https://doi.org/10.1016/S0140-6736(21)00625-5
Singer, M. (2009). *Introduction to Syndemics: A Critical Systems Approach to Public and Community Health*. John Wiley & Sons.
Singer, M., & Baer, H. (2018). *Critical Medical Anthropology*. Routledge.
Smith, D. E. (1989). Feminist reflections on political economy. *Studies in Political Economy*, *30*(1), 37–59.
Stevano, S., Franz, T., Dafermos, Y., & Van Waeyenberge, E. (2021). COVID-19 and crises of capitalism: intensifying inequalities and global responses. *Canadian Journal of Development Studies/Revue canadienne d'études du développement*, *42*(1–2), 1–17.
The Care Collective. (2020). *The Care Manifesto*. Verso.
The Independent Panel for Pandemic Preparedness & Response. (2021). *COVID-19: Make It the Last Pandemic*. https://theindependentpanel.org/wp-content/uploads/2021/05/COVID-19-Make-it-the-Last-Pandemic_final.pdf
The New York Times. (2021). What to know about India's coronavirus crisis. *The New York Times*. www.nytimes.com/article/india-coronavirus-cases-deaths.html
Thomson, K. (2020). By the light of the corona (virus): revealing hegemonic masculinity and the double bind for men in responding to crises. *Health Sociology Review*, *29*(2), 149–157.
Treviño, A. J., Harris, M. A., & Wallace, D. (2008). What's so critical about critical race theory? *Contemporary Justice Review*, *11*(1), 7–10.
Trott, B. (2020). Queer Berlin and the Covid-19 crisis: a politics of contact and ethics of care. *Interface: A Journal for and about Social Movements*, *12*(1), 88–108.
van Kessel, P., Baronavski, C., Scheller, A., & Smith, A. (2021). In their own words, Americans describe the struggles and silver linings of the COVID-19 pandemic. *Pew Research Center*. www.pewresearch.org/2021/03/05/in-their-own-words-americans-describe-the-struggles-and-silver-linings-of-the-covid-19-pandemic/

Yadav, U. N., Rayamajhee, B., Mistry, S. K., Parsekar, S. S., & Mishra, S. K. (2020). A syndemic perspective on the management of non-communicable diseases amid the COVID-19 pandemic in low- and middle-income countries. *Frontiers in Public Health*, *8*(508). www.frontiersin.org/article/10.3389/fpubh.2020.00508

Yarrow, E., & Pagan, V. (2020). Reflections on frontline medical work during Covid-19, and the embodiment of risk. *Gender, Work & Organization*, *28*(S1), 89–100.

3
THE BIOPOLITICS OF COVID
Foucauldian approaches

Introduction

Outbreaks of infectious diseases involve interventions at both macropolitical and micropolitical levels. As I have shown in Chapter 2, these interventions forge significant tensions between individual freedoms and societal benefits, and between protecting population health while simultaneously worsening socioeconomic inequalities. Measures from state authorities and other social institutions and organisations are required to intervene in the transmission of pathogens and collect information about citizens' bodies and activities to document the spread of contagion and assess how well strategies of containment are working. Citizens, for their part, are expected to commit to and observe state-imposed rules for their own good and that of the populace in general, even when their autonomy, freedom of movement and potentially their livelihoods and well-being are significantly restricted.

This chapter uses perspectives drawn from the scholarship of the French historian and philosopher Michel Foucault to trace the historical underpinnings of contemporary approaches and responses to the COVID-19 crisis. Analyses engaging with Foucault's scholarship on the discourses and practices of modes of power, biopolitics and governmentality focus on the political dimensions of how social groups and populations (the 'body politic') as well as individual bodies ('the care of the self') are managed, disciplined and governed. Various levels of control over citizens' bodies and movements are exerted and rationales for limiting individual freedoms put forward for protecting the health of the body politic. Foucauldian theory offers concepts for understanding these tensions and relations of power. The related work on biopolitics of philosophers Giorgio Agamben, Roberto Esposito and Achille Mbembe is also discussed: including their analyses of the COVID crisis.

Modes of power, care of the self and the governance of citizens

Michel Foucault was interested in the relationships between the operation of power, the generation and practice of knowledge about human experiences and life, identities and social institutions. Foucault's philosophy differs from Marxist historical materialism (Chapter 2) in that while he acknowledges the materialities of embodiment, place and space, he places more emphasis on ideas, language and discourse. Foucault does not posit a hierarchy between materialities as coming first and concepts emerging from these materialities, as historical materialism would have it.

Foucault's theorising also differed from Marxist thought in that he did not position power relations as always repressive and exerted by the ruling classes over the working classes. Rather than seeing power as an economic resource foremost, Foucault positioned it as a web of relations and knowledge, involving complex intersections between materialities, discourses and ideologies. For Foucault, modern forms of power are largely productive rather than repressive, generating new knowledge, norms and practices that can contribute to societal wellbeing as well as to wealth and authority. He argued that while strategies and discourses wielded by modern democracies can at times be coercive, violent and limiting of people's agency (as exemplified by the criminal justice system or immigration restrictions), they are exercised for a range of other more benign purposes, including improving citizens' well-being, health and life expectancy.

Foucault positioned power as a dynamic set of relationships that existed in every encounter, evident in three main modes. Sovereign power is the traditional repressive form, involving coercion, punishment and even the killing of citizens by the ruling class. It is the right to take life or let live. Disciplinary power involves the mobilisation and control of people's bodies and capacities for the benefit of themselves as well as the state, often involving social institutions and expert knowledge. The newest mode of power is biopower: exercised with and through populations in the interests of the governance of citizens' productivity, health and welfare. Foucault argued that while sovereign power dominated regimes and practices of authority in pre-Enlightenment eras in Europe, from the seventeenth century the focus gradually turned towards enhancing and supporting human life through population surveillance and administration as part of disciplinary and biopower. In so doing, the state became increasingly involved in the private lives of its citizens, but in ways that were far less coercive or repressive but rather encouraged them to internalise and conform to dominant norms and expectations.

In his analytical and historical scholarship, Foucault was interested in identifying the norms and expectations associated with disciplinary and biopower and how they intersected with the materialities of place and space. He was also interested in how concepts of selfhood and embodiment are structured through norms, discourses and expectations. Foucault (1986, 1988) explained that the care of the self involves practices and moral laws concerning ethical self-cultivation and self-examination. He (1988) referred to such practices as the 'technologies of the self'. Engaging in the technologies of the self involves seeking out and employing knowledge and the constant making of choices, including conducting monitoring of one's body and activities. Later essays focused on governmentality or the forms by which biopower was generated and exercised in the interest of the public good using the authority of expert knowledge systems and institutions such as medicine and public health (Foucault, 1984, 1991).

In his books *Madness and Civilization* (Foucault, 1965), *Birth of the Clinic* (Foucault, 1975) and *Discipline and Punish* (Foucault, 1977), Foucault focused in particular on the institutions of the prison, the asylum and the medical clinic and hospital and how people's bodies were monitored, measured and disciplined in these institutional spaces. For Foucault (1975), it is through the medical gaze that the patient's body is constructed as a particular archetype of illness. Foucault's work included several references to the use of spatial forms of confinement such as quarantine in dealing with infectious disease. A section of *Discipline and Punish* (Foucault, 1977), for example, goes into detail about public health orders in response to a plague outbreak in a town in the seventeenth century. These measures included locking the gates of the town so that no one could enter or leave and the imposition of the death penalty for people who disobeyed the order to stay inside their homes. Foucault notes how rigid this disciplinary form of power was, confining every individual to their space, risking their lives, contagion or punishment if they were caught. In these cases, the medical gaze becomes the public health gaze but with a far more carceral orientation. People are watched not for their own benefit but for that of their communities. Foucault views such a state of surveillance and control as the ideal of the perfectly governed city, where everyone knows what is expected of them to protect the public health. It is the precursor to modern forms of biopower exercised as part of public health surveillance and infection control.

Bringing together the ideas of technologies of the self with systems of governmentality, Foucault emphasised that states' strategies for the management of populations predominantly operate to encourage citizens to conform to dominant ideas about self-responsibility and management of their own lives for their own flourishing. As he observed, in contemporary democratic societies, governments mostly manage their populations by attempting to persuade them to promote their own best interests, helping them to become productive and ideal citizens of the state. While Marxists are primarily interested in the macropolitics of the operation of power, therefore, Foucault focused on the micropolitics: the everyday moments in which citizens choose to conform to (or resist) the dominant discourses and practices to which they have been acculturated as part of the societies in which they live. He argued that people are encouraged to internalise norms of behaviour and care of their bodies as part of this acculturation, so that they become docile bodies. They are not always docile, however, and can directly reject or reinvent these norms and expectations.

Foucauldian analyses of medicine and public health

Scholars building on Foucault's scholarship on disciplinary power and biopower to write about contemporary medical and public health practices have observed that in cultures of the Global North, the body is viewed as signifying the self and demonstrating an individual's capacity for self-knowledge, self-mastery and self-care. Under the discourse of self-control, citizens are urged to turn the medical gaze upon themselves and engage in such technologies of the self as monitoring their own bodies and health states and taking preventive action in accordance with medical and public health directives. Public health measures for dealing with infectious and other diseases rest identifying risk behaviours and risky places as well as the social groups who most vulnerable to contracting and spreading a disease (Lupton, 1995; Petersen & Lupton, 1996). Particularly since the rise of epidemiological surveillance of populations in the eighteenth century as a biopolitical initiative (Foucault, 1984), these strategies have been employed to assist in collecting, archiving, processing and displaying health-related data such as cases of disease and deaths (Armstrong, 1995) as well as for infectious disease management efforts such as contact tracing during epidemics (Kahn, 2020).

The Italian philosopher Georgio Agamben is well known for his scholarship on the biopolitics and governmentality of what he describes as 'bare life': particularly in his most well-known book in the Anglophone world, *Homo Sacer: Sovereign Power and Bare Life* (Agamben, 1995). In this and other works, Agamben seeks to re-establish sovereign power as a form of biopolitics. Agamben draws a distinction between bare life, or *zoe*, and *bios*, the political and ethical dimensions of human experience. Bare life, according to Agamben, refers to the biological, fleshly dimensions of the human body and its health states, devoid of any social, political or cultural meanings or human rights. He outlines what he terms the 'states of exception', determined by the holders of sovereign power, which reduce certain people to bare life, depriving them of their civil liberties. In states of exception (which may include crises such as wars, natural disasters and pandemics), usual constitutional rights of citizens can be ignored or flouted in the interests of protecting the public good. Disciplinary power and biopower are superseded by sovereign power, with the state and its associated institutions acting as the sovereign. These authorities exert coercive and repressive forms of power on social groups they consider to be less deserving of status as free individuals and the bearer of human rights, such as refugees confined to camps. Rather than a political economy distinction between social classes, therefore, Agamben makes a distinction between those social groups who are considered in terms only of bare life and those who are accorded the full human rights and status of citizens.

Prior to the emergence of COVID, Roberto Esposito, another Italian philosopher, had outlined what he described as an affirmative biopolitics, compared with what he characterised as the negative biopolitics of Agamben's writings. In his books *Bios: Biopolitics and Philosophy* (Esposito, 2008) and *Immunitas: The Protection and*

Negation of Life (Esposito, 2011), Esposito uses the term 'immunity' as a metaphor for the protection of the body politic. For Esposito, immunity mechanisms (conceived of broadly as state-based systems for protecting their citizens) contribute to a mode of sovereign power used to protect a community against threats, both internal and external, and to maintain the borders between inside and outside. In this conceptualisation, Esposito's debt to Mary Douglas' scholarship on risk and danger (discussed further in Chapter 4) is evident. He sought to demonstrate how late modern ideas about immunity position it as a conceptual framework for understanding social and political control. He identified tensions between living in a community and protecting its members from threats to their health and life with the use of immunitary mechanisms.

Esposito argued that departing from medieval concepts of danger founded on Christian belief, practices of immunity began to develop in post-Enlightenment Europe. These strategies were initiated by the state to protect societies from disease and other risks, such as conflict and civil unrests. Such immunitary mechanisms include the institution of public health as well as the legal, policing and security systems. Esposito's ideas about the biopolitics of immunity mechanisms are more affirmative than Agamben. He sees these approaches as contributing to the health and safety of societies, including limiting the spread and effects of infectious diseases. However, Esposito also acknowledges that immunitary mechanisms can be taken too far: to the point that they can begin to harm the community they are implemented to protect by generating another set of harms and dangers, such as severe restrictions on citizens' freedoms.

Other scholars engaging with Foucault's work have noted that biopolitical discourses and practices can operate to make distinctions between what forms of human life are considered to be worthy of protection or the right to survival and flourishing. In his book *Necropolitics* (Mbembe 2019), Cameroonian philosopher Achille Mbembe focuses on the biopolitics of death rather than life (the prefix 'necro' refers to death or the corpse). While Foucault's scholarship on disciplinary and biopower focused on how state agencies and expert knowledge were directed at monitoring and promoting human life, Mbembe points out that these modes of power can also be used to regulate human death, to create 'death-worlds'. In particular, Mbembe highlights how racism and colonialism have come together with biopolitics to configure the bodies of people of colour as less worthy of life – indeed as less human – than those of white people, simply because of their race. As Mbembe argues, the right to decide who lives and who dies is the ultimate expression of biopolitics: enshrined not only in legal institutions, capitalist economic systems, militarisation and colonialism but also in public health and social welfare policies and practices. These strategies of power may not necessarily involve the direct threatening of life that was common to sovereign power. Instead, they can operate indirectly to position certain human lives as less important than others, rationalising the withdrawing or limiting of support for them and thereby exposing some people to the heightened risk of death.

Biopolitical analyses of the COVID crisis

During the COVID crisis, physical confinement, policing and surveillance measures employed in quarantine and social isolation measures have combined time-honoured methods such as isolation and border control with digital technologies for monitoring people's movements and geolocation. These strategies involve the coming together of practices at a national or regional level with the everyday activities and habits of their citizens. Together with the expectations of citizens that they voluntarily police and regulate themselves by avoiding coronavirus infection adopting recommended measures (hand and cough hygiene, physical distancing, mask wearing, vaccination), in many countries there was direct implementation of sovereign as well as disciplinary and biopower.

Government responses often combined zealous policing of public spaces such as parks and beaches and national or regional borders with exhortations to citizens to practice prevention measures for the good of everyone as well as for their own protection from infection. Special powers were implemented by governments to police and control their citizens, including closure of international borders, refusing permission to leave or enter the country and fining people who did not obey social distancing or quarantining regulations. On numerous occasions, people were publicly shamed in government press conferences and the news media for flouting public health orders, even when these actions were accidental. Once effective vaccines against COVID became available, some jurisdictions began to mandate vaccination for groups such as hospital or care home workers or demanded proof of vaccination or COVID immunity before people were allowed to enter public places, use public transport or travel across national borders.

As the COVID crisis unfolded, quantification and modelling to generate predictions of how COVID might spread if unchecked were vitally important to public health knowledge and government policies (Milan & Treré, 2020; Rhodes et al., 2020). These metrics are themselves dependent on factors such as COVID testing rates and accuracy, the ways that COVID deaths are identified and categorised, and efficient reporting of cases and mortality: all strategies that have become highly politicised. For example, former US President Trump was notorious for making public pronouncements about wanting to slow down COVID testing rates in the USA so that the country's case statistics would not appear as dire (ABC News Online, 2020). Authoritarian and corrupt governments have been called to account for continual under-testing and under-reporting of COVID cases and mortality rates, while other countries simply do not have the resources to offer comprehensive COVID testing (Milan & Treré, 2020).

Governments have differed significantly in the extent to which they have monitored their citizens or imposed strict regulations. These differences have not always been aligned along political ideological approaches. Building on a long history of state-based control over citizens' bodies and health (including the one-child policy), the authoritarian Chinese Communist Party's administration was among the most restrictive in dealing with the pandemic. Beginning very early in the pandemic with the 'ground zero' city of Wuhan, severe lockdowns have been regularly implemented in cities and regions, allowing citizens very little opportunity to leave their homes. Militia and guards have been stationed along internal and international borders to prevent movements. Some outbreaks have resulted in mass testing programmes of tens of millions of Chinese citizens. These strongly enforced restrictions, together with extensive contact tracing assisted by digital monitoring systems and strict hotel quarantine for international arrivals, have helped China contain the spread of SARs-CoV-2 very effectively compared with many other nations, despite its massive population and geographical area (Lu et al., 2021; Smith, 2021).

The neoliberal democratic state and federal governments of Australia also imposed prolonged restrictive regulations from early on in the pandemic, with the intention of eliminating SARS-CoV-2, despite operating with very different political ideologies from the Chinese Communist Party. Police officers regularly patrolled and policed borders between states or areas within cities that have been designated as COVID hotspots. Australians have been fined by police for disobeying government orders to stay at home or remain in their defined localities, not physically distancing in public spaces or even sitting to consume takeaway food on a park bench rather than return straight home to eat it. By contrast, most democratic countries globally have adopted mitigation strategies that have adopted a more libertarian stance in seeking to balance citizens' freedoms with controlling COVID spread, including, perhaps most notoriously, the UK, Brazil, India and the USA (as discussed in Chapter 2). Especially in the case of low-income countries with fragile health systems, high levels of socioeconomic disadvantage, experiencing political instability and dominated by populist leaders, such as Brazil and India, these approaches have led to among the highest per capita COVID cases and deaths in the world (Lu et al., 2021; Ruppel et al., 2021).

Once it became obvious that the UK government's early laissez faire approach to COVID policy was a deadly ploy that could not be sustained (Chapter 2), it did introduce lockdowns and strong restrictions on people's movements. However, the UK government continued with a largely libertarian approach to the management of COVID well into 2021, as encapsulated in Prime Minister Boris Johnson's description of removing all COVID legal restrictions in England on 19 July 2021 in time for the European summer as 'freedom day' (Hawke, 2021). Even with the Delta variant causing new increases in COVID cases, Johnson was determined to relax all restrictions on UK citizens' movements, much to the concern of public health experts (Hawke, 2021). Johnson and his government ministers emphasised the importance of citizens to assess their own risk and take responsibility for managing it, rather than relying on government instructions or orders. As medical historian Mark Honigsbaum (2021) observed in an opinion piece for *The Guardian*:

> The exhortation to 'learn to live with Covid' casts each one of us as part moral philosopher, part health economist, making finely tuned decisions about what is an acceptable risk and our responsibility to our fellow citizens ... it's an ethical minefield.

Such an approach to COVID management, from a Foucauldian perspective, demonstrates a classic approach to the governance of populations in response to a health threat to move away from sovereign power to relying on disciplinary power at the level of the individual, assuming they will engage in responsible health-managing citizens as ethical technologies of the self.

The COVID crisis is the first pandemic to be monitored, measured and controlled with the assistance of the latest digital technologies, involving an extensive expansion of disease surveillance, control and communication measures. Alerts about disease cases or exposure sites can be readily disseminated within minutes across the world with the use of expert public health networks together with online news reporting and social media commentary. Live online dashboards such as that offered by WHO and national health authorities provide regularly updated metrics of global numbers of COVID cases, deaths and vaccinations, which can be broken down into regions, countries or local areas, even down to the level of city suburbs. Contact tracing efforts are supplemented by smartphone apps and QR check-in codes that monitor people's movements outside their homes (Lupton, 2022).

Surveillance technology companies have stepped in to offer services that appear to solve the 'problem' of the pandemic in the interests of public health. New systems have been introduced with little warning or public scrutiny and debate. These new services have included rebranding cameras designed to detect weapons as thermal scanners supposedly to detect COVID infections and the use of drones to detect people not conforming to physical distancing or quarantine regulations. Such digitised surveillance strategies are redolent of the measures that are used in the criminal justice system, where employing electronic monitoring technologies such as digital tracking bands has been a feature of controlling offenders' movements once released from a custodial sentence, or even in warfare, as in the case of surveillance drones (Graham & McIvor, 2017).

In some locations, digital technologies and digital data analytics were taken up as ways of tracking people's location and movements to ensure that they adhere to self-isolation restrictions for the length of the quarantine period. For example, in China, people were prevented from leaving their homes if they had been identified as infected with COVID by a digitised rating system on an Alipay or WeChat phone app that coded them 'red' and therefore as required to go into quarantine (Zhou, 2020). Nationally mandated location tracking apps to monitor the movements of citizens were introduced in Qatar, India, Russia and Poland. People in some of these countries were denied entry to businesses, government offices or public transport unless they could demonstrate that they had checked in using the app (Gershgorn,

2021). South Korea, Israel, Hong Kong and Taiwan deployed similar tools for surveillance of the movements of people who had been diagnosed with COVID, their contacts and other people ordered to be in quarantine, including those newly arrived from overseas. South Korea used an app that informed potential contacts of an infected person, while Hong Kong issued incoming travellers with tracking bracelets (Calvo et al., 2020).

Even in Western neoliberal jurisdictions, people's digital privacy has been flouted on numerous occasions in the name of public health measures. For example, in June 2021, Australian travellers flying between different Australian states were forced by police to show them their location data on their smartphones or their bank records on online banking apps to prove that they had not been in government-identified COVID hotspots (Lamb & Bartholomew, 2021).

Facial recognition systems were also used in some countries for COVID surveillance. In some Chinese cities, local government authorities implemented monitoring measures using facial recognition data and smartphone data tracking combined with information derived by requesting people to enter details about their health and travel history into online forms when visiting public places (Goh, 2020). Russia introduced facial recognition systems early in the pandemic, deployed by police to identify and fine people who have broken regulations about self-isolation and physical distancing (AlgorithmWatch, 2020). Russian authorities also compelled people who have tested positive for COVID to install a geolocation tracking app, entitled 'Social Monitoring', that sent notifications every two hours, even throughout the night, for the user to upload a selfie to prove they were at home. People who fail to comply with these demands were issued with fines. A similar app was used in Poland (Gershgorn, 2021). Major national border and immigration control systems, including along the US–Mexican border, the Myanmar–Thai border and in the Mediterranean region, began to use COVID as an excuse for introducing more extensive automated surveillance systems such as facial recognition to prevent entry of migrants and refugee-seekers (Venkataramakrishnan, 2021).

Most digital systems have been designed with socioeconomically privileged users from the Global North in mind, thereby ignoring the specific needs and unintended consequences for less-privileged communities and populations. As is the case with traditional public health measures, the civil liberties and autonomy of those deemed to be infected or at risk of infection are in tension with public health goals to control epidemics and pandemics. Academic researchers and civil society groups have drawn attention to the issues with human rights and 'function creep' possibilities of these technologies, including the lack of protection of personal data, transparency about how authorities are currently using this information and plan to do so in the future and the inability of people to challenge the decisions made by the algorithms (AlgorithmWatch, 2020; Calvo et al., 2020; Kahn, 2020; Milan & Treré, 2020).

Agamben and Esposito on COVID

Giorgio Agamben adopted an extreme critique of state-based strategies against COVID early in the crisis. In his short essay first published in Italian in February 2020 and then translated into English under the title 'The Invention of an Epidemic' (Agamben, 2020a), Agamben made some controversial statements arguing against the use of strong measures to contain COVID. Drawing on his previous work on states of exception and bare life, Agamben argued that the Italian government and news media were overreacting to the threat of the pandemic by advocating for what he considered to be overly harsh and restrictive approaches to population surveillance and control. Agamben viewed these pandemic measures as natural extensions of contemporary disciplinary power and biopower that were usually hidden but had readily emerged once COVID has been defined as a state of exception. He criticised the Italian government for deploying measures such as lockdowns, which in his view unnecessarily restricted citizens' freedoms in the name of a health emergency that he considered to be invented rather than a real crisis. Agamben argued that COVID was simply a minor outbreak like seasonal influenza but that the Italian government, in its totalitarian desire for power over its citizens, was using the pandemic as a foil.

In a later essay, entitled 'Clarifications' (Agamben, 2020b), Agamben doubled down on some of his claims. He argued that the Italian response to the COVID crisis, both by the government and by citizens, was panicked, highlighting that bare life is often used by the state as a justification for prioritising health over freedom. According to Agamben, a reduction of human life to bare life was taking place during the pandemic in ways that divided rather than united people. Agamben claimed that a sense of community had been lost as people have been encouraged to see each other as sources of contagion rather than as fellow citizens or family members. He asked, 'what is a society that has no value other than survival?'. For Agamben, the Italian state had convinced its citizens that 'The enemy isn't somewhere inside, it's inside us'.

Agamben's assertions can be viewed as ignoring the subtleties of Foucault's writings on disciplinary power and biopolitics in adopting an overly extreme critique of state interventions to manage COVID. Agamben was quickly subjected to criticism on the part of other scholars (e.g. Peters, 2020) for denying the reality of the pandemic spread in Italy. This country was one of the earliest to be crippled by a raging outbreak that severely strained its health services and the capacities of healthcare workers, leading to deaths that a better prepared system would have been able to prevent. Despite his attempts at clarification of his argument, Agamben's claims still appear hyperbolic. It is difficult to see why the Italian government would want to 'invent' a crisis to justify a strong approach to an outbreak of infectious disease simply to demonstrate its capacity for control over its citizens, particularly given the significant disruptions to everyday life and the economy caused by the imposition of pandemic restrictions in Italy and elsewhere. Indeed, the Italian and other governments (e.g. those of the UK, Brazil, India, Sweden and USA) have been roundly criticised by public health experts and their national news media for not acting quickly enough to introduce strong restrictions on their citizens' movements and therefore losing control of the pandemic's spread (Peters, 2020).

Agamben's critique focuses too heavily on the coercive and disciplinary dimensions of state interventions without recognising their productive capacities: to generate new knowledge about catastrophes such as COVID and to use these to protect both human lives and the economy. Notably, such a position on government restrictions has been echoed in the views of dissenters who have adopted a radical right-wing critique on what they see as the overly coercive actions of 'big government'. These libertarian views have been expressed by people involved in street protests and rallies against governments' COVID lockdown restrictions, vaccination policies and face mask mandates in Agamben's own country, Italy, as well as in the USA, France, Israel, UK, Australia, India, Germany, Ireland, Argentina and elsewhere.

A very different perspective was offered by Roberto Esposito (2020), who also penned some reflections on the COVID very early in the pandemic. He began his essay with noting that he wanted to return to the ancient Latin expression *vitam institutere* (meaning 'institute life') in analysing the impacts of the COVID crisis. Esposito claimed that at a time at which human life appeared to be threatened more than ever, the common effort needed to be directed towards re-instituting life in novel ways, for: 'What else is life, after all, if not an ongoing institution, the ability to always create new significances?'. Like Agamben, Esposito uses the term 'bare life', which he defines as 'mere survival'. However, his argument is that human life can never be reduced to bare life, because from the moment of birth, human life is always social and political. For Esposito, the COVID crisis threatens to break this symbolic network of social and political relations. While staying alive is the first challenge mounted to humans by the pandemic, maintaining social life (the instituted life) is the second one. Unlike Agamben, Esposito thinks that limiting face-to-face social encounters to protect bare life is justifiable in the present moment of crisis. He does emphasise that the importance of social relationships and community feeling needs to be protected as much as possible in the process. One way to achieve this, Esposito argues, is for the loneliness of physical isolation to be given a communal meaning, so that people are united by the shared experience of being alone. He claims that this way of viewing social experience is currently the only viable way of instituting life.

In an interview in an online academic journal appearing in June 2020 (Esposito et al., 2020), Esposito further outlined how his scholarship could be applied to understanding the biopolitics of the COVID crisis. He pointed out that the word 'immunity' had been used continuously from the beginning of the pandemic and that 'We are all seeking immunity in one sense or another'. While vaccination is an obvious practice to develop immunity against infection, practices such as physical isolating and face mask wearing are also part of an 'immunitarian attitude towards human interaction'. Esposito observed that there is even an Italian COVID smartphone app for contact tracing that was titled 'Immuni' (meaning 'immune' in English).

While acknowledging the socioeconomic and emotional tolls associated with severe COVID-related restrictions, Esposito therefore supported the role of the state in implementing and enforcing lockdowns and border closures on citizens' freedoms to protect their health. He was trenchantly critical of governments who attempted a libertarian approach in supporting the concept of herd immunity by allowing SARS-CoV-2 to spread unchecked in their countries: 'Let's say that my assessment of herd immunity is a rather negative one: it acts as a form of autoimmune disease, that is, it tries to protect life through the death of a part of the population'. Esposito argued that a fine balance needed to be struck between keeping people apart from each other as part of immunity mechanisms and preserving their social bonds. He noted that medicine and public health have become even more politicised in the wake of COVID, while politics has become medicalised, treating citizens like patients requiring medical care and protection as a systemic form of immunity. These approaches, according to Esposito, are not an affirmative form of biopolitics. He sees the provision of social support, the provision of better living conditions, attention to protecting the environment and equitable and inclusive access to pharmaceuticals and healthcare as more beneficial in countering the social and economic effects of the COVID crisis than individualistic approaches to protecting and preserving human life.

COVID necropolitics

Writing about the necropolitics of COVID in a brief essay, Achille Mbembe (2021) argued that fears about the COVID crisis are centred on the vulnerability and exposure to contamination and decay of the body. For those living in privileged conditions in the Global North, acknowledging these realities can be emotionally confronting. As Mbembe (2021, p. S59) observed in relation to the global response to COVID:

> It is one thing to worry about the death of others in a distant land and quite another to suddenly become aware of one's own putrescence, to be forced to live intimately with one's own death, contemplating it as a real possibility. Such is, for many, the terror triggered by confinement: having to finally answer for one's own life, to one's own name.

Mbembe suggested that rather than make people more aware of their shared experiences with other humans and the nonhuman world, these fears can easily lead to even greater disavowal of the injustices and inequalities faced by less-privileged social groups in the interests of achieving one's own survival.

As I have described in previous chapters and earlier in this chapter, there is abundant evidence of such responses on the part of political leaders across a variety of political systems: from authoritarian regimes to neoliberal democracies. Other scholars (Jagannathan & Rai, 2021; Messerschmidt, 2020; Sandset, 2021) have taken up Mbembe's original ideas to examine the necropolitics of the COVID crisis in the context of global health inequalities, including those experienced by racialised groups and other marginalised and disadvantaged groups, such as those from the working class, religious minority groups, people with disabilities and LGBTQI people, as well as refugees and displaced people. These scholars have pointed out that during the COVID crisis, members of these social groups were continually positioned and treated as more disposable and expendable than were members of elite and privileged groups.

Once COVID had emerged and begun to spread, the crisis narrative that dominated news reporting of the COVID pandemic in many countries, including neoliberal democracies, related to the crisis of sovereignty. The conditions of austerity and gradual withdrawal of the welfare state in these countries had already exposed these vulnerable social groups to poorer health and shorter life expectancies due to substandard living conditions and poverty. These citizens were therefore hit doubly hard when their governments failed to provide enough financial and social support and healthcare during the COVID crisis. Across the world, many of the people working on the 'frontline' in essential services were those from already socioeconomically disadvantaged groups: immigrants, people of colour, those living in conditions of low income or poverty. Healthcare workers, cleaners and people working in meat-processing plants, supermarkets and delivery services, many of whom existed on a low income with few sick leave benefits, were exposed to the novel coronavirus at a much higher rate than were others who could isolate and work from home (The Independent Panel for Pandemic Preparedness & Response, 2021).

As described in Chapter 2, people of colour in wealthy countries such as the UK and USA were disproportionately exposed to viral infection and consequently experienced greater death rates. Racial/ethnic minorities in countries of the Global South have also borne the brunt of necropolitics. For example, in Brazil, slum dwellers, rural communities and forest dwellers, Indigenous people, Afro-Brazilian and other racialised groups suffered the most under President Bolsano's 'hands off policy' of downplaying the risk of COVID to Brazilians, which has also been described as 'live and let die'. Bolsano and his government had long positioned these groups as less than human, neglecting their welfare for the sake of economic development and better opportunities for the wealthy to the extent that they have been accused of genocide (Russo Lopes & Bastos Lima, 2020).

Race riots and 'Black Lives Matter' protests in response to the police murder of George Floyd in the US city of Minneapolis, June 2020, raised tensions around the need for citizens to protest against the state amid state-imposed orders concerning large public gatherings in response to COVID. In several liberal democratic countries in which these protests occurred, including Australia and the UK as well as the USA, long-established freedoms to politically protest and gather peaceably in public for activist purposes in support of the lives of people of colour clashed with COVID-based restrictions to protect the public's health. While the 'Black Lives Matter' protests were specifically in relation to police brutality against people of colour in the USA, more broadly they challenged the necropolitical and colonial ethics of disposability that have characterised the US approach to Black lives from the years of slavery until the modern-day response to COVID, serving to highlight the intersectional biopolitics of race, health and policing (Schaffer, 2020).

The early months of the pandemic saw a rush on diagnostic tests, pharmaceuticals, oxygen supplies, medical equipment such as respirators to ventilate people with serious COVID-related breathing difficulties and personal protective equipment to protect healthcare workers. Many countries were caught short as a global shortage began to occur in the rush to acquire these supplies and did not have stockpiles put aside on which they could draw. Supply chains were disrupted by border closures and factory closedowns due to COVID lockdown restrictions. Hoarding, price gouging and fraud resulted across the world, as health systems became desperate to maintain or increase their supplies of these essential products. These shortages resulted in a high death toll of healthcare workers in badly affected countries, as they simply did not have enough protective equipment. Healthcare workers were placed under enormous stress in countries with very high cases in hospital, and health systems were not equipped to deal with a prolonged crisis. The needs of people with chronic health conditions or needing medical attention for acute conditions as well as those in care homes for older people were often neglected (The Independent Panel for Pandemic Preparedness & Response, 2021).

Schaffer (2020, p. 46) describes this approach as a 'kind of societal triage', in which people considered to be most worthy of protection from viral infection and death from COVID are typically white, wealthy, young and able-bodied, professional people who can easily work from home. Those who do not meet these priority criteria are treated as more expendable: denied adequate healthcare or sent out to work on 'essential' but low-paid infrastructural support jobs.

The politics of vaccine distribution are a further example of necropolitics at work. High-income nations have been criticised by organisations such as WHO and the People's Vaccine Alliance for failing to provide enough funding to low-income countries to fairly distribute vaccines. According to the Alliance, an international coalition of campaign bodies, by the end of 2020 wealthy countries had purchased enough vaccines to immunise their own populations at least three times over. High-income nations represented only 14% of the world's population but had bought over half of the most promising vaccines at that point in time. The People's Vaccine Alliance subsequently called on all the pharmaceutical companies who were working on vaccines to share their intellectual property so that vaccine production could be ramped up (Anonymous, 2020).

In January 2021, the head of WHO, Tedros Adhanom Ghebreyesus, asserted that the world faced 'a catastrophic more failure' with 'the price of this failure [to be] paid with lives and livelihoods in the world's poorest countries' due to inequities around vaccine production and distribution. He went on to argue that a 'me first' attitude, as evinced in high-income countries, was not fair: healthy young people in such countries had been able to be immunised before more vulnerable people in low-income states. Meanwhile, restricting access to vaccines would lead to increasing prices and hoarding, while the pandemic continued to spread unabated in countries with little access. WHO supported the participation of member states in the global vaccine-sharing scheme COVAX, which began operation in early 2021 (Anonymous, 2021).

Even within wealthy countries, there can be marked disparities between vaccination status. The city of New York provides one example. In July 2021, while 52% full vaccination of its residents had been achieved, there were major differences between parts of the city. While 98% of people living in the high-income financial district of the city had been fully vaccinated, in most parts of Central Brooklyn, a far more socioeconomically diverse area, only one third had received two doses (Bellafante, 2021). Community leaders suggested that people from disadvantaged social groups had high levels of anxiety about COVID vaccines, generated from their life experiences of financial precarity, marginalisation and neglect of their needs coupled with coercive interventions into their private lives on the part of the healthcare and social welfare systems in their city. These feelings should not be characterised as demonstrating 'hesitancy' about or 'resistance' to vaccination. They are founded on people's realistic distrust of authorities and concerns about how they would pay the bills or care for their children if they experience side effects from the vaccines (Bellafante, 2021).

Critics engaging with the concept of necropolitics have pointed out that prior to and during the crisis, health inequalities were largely accepted in authoritarian governments but also neoliberal democracies such as the UK, USA, Canada, Australia, New Zealand and throughout western Europe. The neoliberal approach to healthcare provision in those countries had over several decades created an environment that led not to the saving of lives or improvement of health for marginalised social groups but rather slow violence and death by neglect. These conditions of slow death are endemic rather than epidemic. They are not crises; they are continuing slow-motion conditions of violence, involving general acceptance by the state that marginalised and disadvantaged social groups will continue to suffer and die in far greater numbers than more privileged groups (Sandset, 2021).

Concluding comments

I have shown in Chapter 2 and this chapter that many governments and national leaders working from neoliberal or libertarian political ideologies have failed adequately to protect their citizens from the health and socioeconomic ill effects of the COVID crisis. The most vulnerable social groups in these countries have been particularly badly affected from lack of due care and protection by governments that wanted to avoid a 'big government' approach and rely on individuals to protect themselves. By contrast, authoritarian regimes, such as that China's Community Party, were able to manage the spread of SARS-CoV-2 comparatively well by implementing and enforcing severe restrictions: albeit at the expense of civil liberties.

All three modes of power described by Foucault have been evident from the early days of the COVID outbreak. Traditional forms of sovereign power have been exercised to limit (in some cases, forcibly) people's movements and confine them in quarantine or their homes. A range of surveillance measures, both digital and non-digital, have come into operation to monitor and measure people's whereabouts and quantify vital metrics such as cases, deaths and vaccination rates. These strategies build on disciplinary measures that have been employed for centuries by government agencies and public health authorities to manage disease outbreaks. Practices of biopower have also been important to the quest to contain COVID, requiring citizens to voluntarily adopt personal hygiene practices, isolate themselves when requested by authorities and accept vaccination when offered. Engagements with Foucauldian scholarship in response to the COVID crisis have veered from commentary that recognises the productive use of the modes of power as the inevitable response of governments in dealing with a prolonged pandemic to writing that views such measures as coercive and limiting of civil liberties.

These forms of power that delimit and prescribe the mobilities and interactions of human bodies have been introduced and justified in terms of managing the risks that COVID poses to both individuals and to the body politic. They represent what I have described as a governmentality approach to risk surveillance and control (Lupton, 2013). In Chapter 4, I discuss risk cultures and practices in greater depth, drawing on the risk society approach developed by Ulrich Beck and the cultural/symbolic perspective outlined in the scholarship of Mary Douglas.

References

ABC News Online. (2020). Donald Trump says he ordered slowdown in coronavirus testing in speech to rally in Tulsa, Oklahoma. *ABC News Online.* www.abc.net.au/news/2020-06-21/donald-trump-says-ordered-slowdown-coronavirus-testing/12377556

Agamben, G. (1995). *Homo Sacer: Sovereign Power and Bare Life.* Stanford University Press.

Agamben, G. (2020a). The invention of an epidemic. *European Journal of Psychoanalysis.* www.journal-psychoanalysis.eu/coronavirus-and-philosophers/

Agamben, G. (2020b). Clarifications. *An Und Für Sich.* https://itself.blog/2020/03/17/giorgio-agamben-clarifications/

AlgorithmWatch. (2020). *Automated Decision-Making Systems in the COVID-19 Pandemic: A European Perspective.* https://algorithmwatch.org/en/automating-society-2020-covid19/

Anonymous. (2020). Rich countries hoarding Covid vaccines, says People's Vaccine Alliance. *BBC News*. www.bbc.com/news/health-55229894

Anonymous. (2021). Covid vaccine: WHO warns of 'catastrophic moral failure'. *BBC News*. www.bbc.com/news/world-55709428

Armstrong, D. (1995). The rise of surveillance medicine. *Sociology of Health & Illness*, 17(3), 393–404.

Bellafante, G. (2021). Free doughnuts aren't going to boost vaccination rates. *The New York Times*. www.nytimes.com/2021/07/09/nyregion/free-doughnuts-arent-going-to-boost-vaccination-rates.html

Calvo, R. A., Deterding, S., & Ryan, R. M. (2020). Health surveillance during COVID-19 pandemic. *British Medical Journal*. 369. www.bmj.com/content/369/bmj.m1373

Esposito, R. (2008). *Bios: Biopolitics and Philosophy*. University of Minnesota Press.

Esposito, R. (2011). *Immunitas: The Protection and Negation of Life*. Polity.

Esposito, R. (2020). Instituting life. *The LA Review of Books*. https://lareviewofbooks.org/article/quarantine-files-thinkers-self-isolation/

Esposito, R., Christiaens, T., & De Cauwer, S. (2020). The biopolitics of immunity in times of COVID-19: an interview with Roberto Esposito. *Antipode Online*. https://antipodeonline.org/2020/06/16/interview-with-roberto-esposito/

Foucault, M. (1965). *Madness and Civilization: The History of Insanity in the Age of Reason*. Random House.

Foucault, M. (1975). *The Birth of the Clinic: An Archaeology of Medical Perception*. Vintage Books.

Foucault, M. (1977). *Discipline and Punish: The Birth of the Prison* (A. Sheridan, Trans.; 2nd ed.). Allen Lane.

Foucault, M. (1984). The politics of health in the eighteenth century. In *The Foucault Reader* (pp. 273–289). Pantheon Books.

Foucault, M. (1986). *The Care of the Self: The History of Sexuality Volume 3*. Pantheon.

Foucault, M. (1988). Technologies of the self. In L. Martin, H. Gutman, & P. Hutton (Eds.), *Technologies of the Self: A Seminar with Michel Foucault* (pp. 16–49). Tavistock.

Foucault, M. (1991). Governmentality. In G. Burchell, C. Gordon, & P. Miller (Eds.), *The Foucault Effect: Studies in Governmentality* (pp. 87–104). Harvester Wheatsheaf.

Gershgorn, D. (2021). Covid-19 ushered in a new era of government surveillance. *One Zero*. https://onezero.medium.com/covid-19-ushered-in-a-new-era-of-government-surveillance-414afb7e4220

Goh, B. (2020). China rolls out fresh data collection campaign to combat coronavirus. *ITNews*. www.itnews.com.au/news/china-rolls-out-fresh-data-collection-campaign-to-combat-coronavirus-538635

Graham, H., & McIvor, G. (2017). Electronic monitoring in the criminal justice system. *Iriss*. www.iriss.org.uk/resources/insights/electronic-monitoring-criminal-justice-system

Hawke, J. (2021). England will soon abandon almost all coronavirus restrictions. The Netherlands shows what could happen next. *ABC News Online*. www.abc.net.au/news/2021-07-18/freedom-day-looms-in-england-despite-coronavirus-surge/100295326

Honigsbaum, M. (2021). History offers little guide to how we should escape from Covid's clutches. *The Guardian*. www.theguardian.com/commentisfree/2021/jul/11/history-offers-little-guide-to-how-we-should-escape-from-covids-clutches

Jagannathan, S., & Rai, R. (2021). The necropolitics of neoliberal state response to the Covid-19 pandemic in India. *Organization*, online first. https://doi.org/10.1177/13505084211020195

Kahn, J. P. (2020). *Digital Contact Tracing for Pandemic Response: Ethics and Governance Guidance*. Johns Hopkins University Press.

Lamb, J., & Bartholomew, K. (2021). Sunshine Coast Airport arrivals confused and angry at police 'invasion of privacy'. *ABC News Online*. www.abc.net.au/news/2021-06-03/covid-19-police-patrol-angers-and-confuses-queensland-travellers/100177988

Lu, G., Razum, O., Jahn, A., Zhang, Y., Sutton, B., Sridhar, D., Ariyoshi, K., von Seidlein, L., & Müller, O. (2021). COVID-19 in Germany and China: mitigation versus elimination strategy. *Global Health Action*, 14(1). www.tandfonline.com/doi/full/10.1080/16549716.2021.1875601

Lupton, D. (1995). *The Imperative of Health: Public Health and the Regulated Body*. Sage.

Lupton, D. (2013). *Risk* (2nd ed.). Routledge.

Lupton, D. (2022). The quantified pandemic: digitised surveillance, containment and care in response to the COVID-19 crisis. In S. Pink, M. Berg, D. Lupton, & M. Ruckenstein (Eds.), *Everyday Automation: Experiencing and Anticipating Automated Decision-Making*. Routledge.

Mbembe, A. (2019). *Necropolitics*. Duke University Press.

Mbembe, A. (2021). The universal right to breathe. *Critical Inquiry*, 47(S2), S58–S62.

Messerschmidt, J. W. (2020). Donald Trump, dominating masculine necropolitics, and COVID-19. *Men and Masculinities*, 24(1), 189–194.

Milan, S., & Treré, E. (2020). The rise of the data poor: the COVID-19 pandemic seen from the margins. *Social Media + Society*, 6(3). https://doi.org/10.1177/2056305120948233

Peters, M. A. (2020). Philosophy and pandemic in the postdigital era: Foucault, Agamben, Žižek. *Postdigital Science and Education*. https://doi.org/10.1007/s42438-020-00117-4

Petersen, A., & Lupton, D. (1996). *The New Public Health: Health and Self in the Age of Risk*. Sage.

Rhodes, T., Lancaster, K., & Rosengarten, M. (2020). A model society: maths, models and expertise in viral outbreaks. *Critical Public Health*, 30(3), 253–256.

Ruppel, A., Halim, M. I., Kikon, R., Mohamed, N. S., & Saebipour, M. R. (2021). Could COVID-19 be contained in poor populations by herd immunity rather than by strategies designed for affluent societies or potential vaccine(s)? *Global Health Action, 14*(1). https://doi.org/10.1080/16549716.2020.1863129

Russo Lopes, G., & Bastos Lima, M. G. (2020). Necropolitics in the jungle: COVID-19 and the Marginalisation of Brazil's Forest Peoples. *Bulletin of Latin American Research, 39*, 92–97.

Sandset, T. (2021). The necropolitics of COVID-19: race, class and slow death in an ongoing pandemic. *Global Public Health, 16*(8–9), 1411–1423.

Schaffer, S. (2020). Necroethics in the time of COVID-19 and Black Lives Matter. In *COVID-19: Volume 1: Global Pandemic, Societal Responses, Ideological Solutions* (pp. 43–53). Routledge.

Smith, M. (2021). Vaccinated but still isolated: China's new virus challenge. *Financial Review*. www.afr.com/world/asia/vaccinated-but-still-isolated-china-s-new-virus-challenge-20210707-p587k7

The Independent Panel for Pandemic Preparedness & Response. (2021). *COVID-19: Make It the Last Pandemic*. https://theindependentpanel.org/wp-content/uploads/2021/05/COVID-19-Make-it-the-Last-Pandemic_final.pdf

Venkataramakrishnan, S. (2021). Algorithms and the coronavirus pandemic. *Financial Times*. www.ft.com/content/16f4ded0-e86b-4f77-8b05-67d555838941

Zhou, V. (2020). How big data is dividing the public in China's coronavirus fight – green, yellow, red. *South China Morning Post*. www.scmp.com/news/china/society/article/3051907/green-yellow-red-how-big-data-dividing-public-chinas-coronavirus

4
RISK AND COVID
Risk society and risk cultures

Introduction

As I have shown in previous chapters, in COVID societies feelings of anxiety and fear about the future are coupled with experiences for many individuals in the present time of significant material hardships, ill health and the death of loved ones. Concepts, understandings and practices related to risk and uncertainty are to the fore in many people's everyday lives, as they struggle to make sense of how the COVID crisis is evolving and how best they should respond to it. The simultaneous invisibility of potentially deadly risk and recognition of the permeability of the body's boundaries can lead to feelings of dread, anxiety and loss of control. These days, the word 'risk' is frequently used as a synonym for an anticipated danger or hazard. These conventions of labelling may on the surface appear 'modern' and 'rational', yet they are often suffused with affective forces that lead to the casting of moral judgements. Individuals, social groups and organisations may be labelled 'at risk', and therefore vulnerable to a threat or danger, or alternatively as themselves 'risky', meaning that they are positioned as posing a threat or harm to others and blamed accordingly for their culpability (Lupton, 2013).

In my book on risk theory (Lupton, 2013), I identified three major theoretical approaches to the social analysis of risk: the 'risk society' approach instigated by sociologist Ulrich Beck's influential book of the same name; the 'cultural/symbolic' perspective, which is based in the structural anthropological scholarship of Mary Douglas; and the

DOI: 10.4324/9781003200512-5

'governmentality' viewpoint, which builds on Foucauldian theory. All three approaches were highly influential in the 1990s and into the early 2000s, when sociocultural and political research on risk was burgeoning. They have been less discussed in recent years due to new topics and theories achieving prominence. However, this scholarship on the sociocultural aspects of risk can be re-invigorated by being used to illuminate how macroprocesses such as reflexive modernisation, cosmopolitanism and individualisation (from Beck's writings), cultures of blame, stigmatisation and symbolic boundary control (drawing on Douglas' writings) and governmentality in the context of biopolitics (key concepts from Foucauldian scholarship) have operated in the COVID crisis. Chapter 3 has already demonstrated how Foucauldian theory can be used to elucidate the biopolitical dimensions of risk in the context of the COVID crisis. The present chapter focuses on Beck's risk society perspective and Douglas' cultural/symbolic approach to risk.

Risk society

The late German sociologist Ulrich Beck's contribution to Anglophone risk theory began with the publication of the English translation of his book *Risk Society: Towards a New Modernity* (Beck, 1992). This publication, which remains his most well known in Anglophone academia, was followed by plethora of other translated volumes in quick succession: among others including *Ecological Politics in an Age of Risk* (Beck, 1995), *World Risk Society* (Beck, 1999), *The Cosmopolitan Vision* (Beck, 2004) and *World at Risk* (Beck, 2009).

As a critical sociologist interested in identifying social inequalities, the sources of political conflict and the role played by social structures and organisations in social change, Beck's writings built on political economy approaches (Chapter 2). His risk society thesis, as it was first outlined in *Risk Society* (Beck, 1992) and then in later books on world risk society (Beck, 1999, 2009), however, reoriented the focus of the Marxian emphasis on social class. Key themes in Beck's risk society scholarship were reflexive modernisation, individualisation and cosmopolitanism. Beck defined reflexive modernisation as a critique of and confrontation with the outcomes of modernisation. He argued that such critiques, including scepticism about the value of expert knowledges and systems and the conviction that late industrial societies are destroying themselves, are major contributors to the character of risk society. Rather than the Marxist critiques that called for overthrows of the class system outlined in Chapter 2, in Beck's view it is this ethos of reflexive modernisation that is the major source of political conflict and change. Individualisation, as described by Beck, is the consequence of traditional expectations and values dissolving. It requires people to take charge of managing and making considered decisions about their own lives rather than following longstanding rules and norms.

The cosmopolitan outlook, as Beck (2004) outlines it, refers to the assumption that boundaries have blurred, regionality has diminished, cultural ties and identities have expanded beyond borders. He proposed that as a consequence of these socioeconomic transformations, many citizens now view themselves as part of a global world community, or as 'world citizens'. According to Beck, this outlook also continues to include elements of nationalism: particularly when contentious issues such as immigration or terrorism are considered. The cosmopolitan outlook is related to reflexive modernisation and individualisation because it involves a self-critical and sceptical awareness of the ambivalences and contradictions of contemporary life: including in relation to risks and uncertainties. Beck proposed that people can veer back and forth between the two perspectives, depending on the context, including retreating into nationalism when they feel threatened.

Beck defined 'risks' as a series of real dangers, uncertainties and hazards that had been selected and identified as 'risks' but also noted that this selection and nomination is historically and culturally contingent. Beck (1995, p. 47) described the selection of phenomena as risks (and the ignoring of others) as a 'cultural disposition': giving the example of dying forests in Germany as receiving a great deal of public attention, while high numbers of car accidents receive far less. Across his writings, Beck argued that while there were not necessarily more risks or uncertainties in the late modern period of the twentieth century compared with previous eras, risk society is characterised by a heightened awareness of risk and of the human contribution to generating risk. He described 'risk society' as characterised by uncertainties and hazards that have become incalculable because of their sheer expansion globally and at large scale. Beck contended that many risks are no longer localised but tend to cross national or regional borders and affect all social groups. This is why he used the term 'world risk society' (Beck, 1999, 2009) in his later writings.

Importantly, Beck drew a distinction between what he defined as the new human-made threats of late modernity and those 'natural disasters' (floods, earthquakes and the like) that have always affected human health and well-being. Beck argued that in past eras, these natural disasters were not viewed as the outcome of human actions but rather as acts of fate or caused by supernatural forces. Therefore, no assignation of responsibility or blame was directed for these crises: they were simply considered to be bad luck. According to Beck, in the current period of late modernity, even these dangers are now considered at least partly caused by humans, as are a panoply of the many other new hazards that the processes of industrialisation and globalisation have set in train.

Another major point in Beck's risk society thesis is that whereas in early industrial societies the focus was on generating and distributing 'goods' such as commodities, employment and wealth, the processes of the late industrial age (such as nuclear power plants, factory farming and other polluting and contaminating industries) were contributing to 'bads' (irreversible threats to human and planetary health and well-being). The expert knowledge institutions of late modernity, such as science and medicine, were viewed as failing to effectively calculate, prevent and manage these risks: these dangers were simply too invisible, too widespread and too difficult to manage. For these risks, it is difficult to identify a single cause or agent who can be blamed for their emergence. Early modern logics of risk attribution and causality therefore have broken down in the face of the globalisation of risk, and publics have become sceptical about the benefits or accuracy of expert knowledges. Consequently, definitions of risk have become even more uncertain and contested. At the same time, as part of the move towards individualisation, publics are expected to seek out knowledge about risks and uncertainties and take action to protect themselves (see also Foucault's concept of technologies of the self in Chapter 3).

Risk society and COVID

Beck's writings on risk focused mostly on ecological and environmental hazards and problems, such as pollution and climate change. Much of his *Risk Society* book, first published in the German original in 1986, was stimulated by the Chernobyl nuclear power plant disaster of that year, which had a severe and long-lasting environmental impact on the country of Ukraine (then part of the former Soviet Union) and other parts of northern and central Europe. Beck's later work on world risk society and cosmopolitanism featured even greater focus on the globalisation of these incalculable risks. He did not discuss the hazards posed by emerging infectious diseases to any great extent even in his latest work (Beck's death pre-dated COVID-19 by five years but his scholarship on risk appeared after the advent of the HIV/AIDS epidemic). However, Beck did discuss health-related issues related to environmental degradation as well as the dangers posed by novel technologies, such as genetically modified foods and genetic cloning and how societies respond to these risks.

Connections can therefore be readily made between Beck's insights on the impact of late modern institutions on the environment and the role played by humans' interventions such as extensive land clearing and mass global travel in the emergence and spread of new zoonotic viruses such as SARS-CoV-2. Pandemics such as COVID are by definition global risks and require global-level responses. They therefore fit Beck's characterisation of world risk society. From this perspective, COVID can be viewed as one of the most recent risks generated by late modernity. Further, like many of the environmental hazards on which Beck's work focused, the novel coronavirus is an invisible threat that is not easily perceptible by the human senses. The sheer intangibility and invisibility of COVID risk – the tiny particles of the coronavirus carried in the air, passed from breath to breath – together with the mutations of the virus that lead to new risks and demand different modes of response, means that the threat becomes even more difficult to understand. Everyday activities and relationships with other people have become fraught with invisible danger.

The threat posed by COVID is also largely incalculable and uncertain, similar to the risks of late modernity described by Beck in his books and other publications. Despite the best efforts of health authorities and governments to monitor cases of infection and deaths from the disease, these metrics have been shown to be inaccurate. As I observed in Chapter 3, in some jurisdictions, authorities have wildly undermeasured cases and deaths for deliberate political reasons or simply because they lack the testing and audit technologies and systems to accurately record these statistics. Time-honoured methods of outbreak control such as quarantine, the closing of international borders and lockdowns in themselves generate ever-more risks: to people's mental health and feelings of well-being, to the economy and social and family relationships. Plans for business or holiday travel have been discarded, as border closures and flight cancellations come into play, with little certainty about when it may be safe again to travel.

While Beck is highly concerned with social justice in his writings on risk, his assertions that the contemporary risks and uncertainties of late modernity have similar effects across geographical regions and social groups are not supported by the overwhelming evidence presented in previous chapters that regions and groups who were already socioeconomically disadvantaged or marginalised have been far more badly affected by the COVID crisis than have more privileged groups and countries. It is also important to note that many of the dangers and uncertainties that have been part of the COVID crisis go well beyond health risks, involving circumstances that could not be anticipated in Beck's risk society scholarship. For example, confining people to their homes for weeks or months on end has been a central strategy of governments to control the spread of the coronavirus. As discussed in previous chapters, while this strategy is effective for the specific purpose of containing infection, it creates other hazards: feelings of loneliness and distress due to loss of social contact, relationship breakdown and family violence, loss of income or unemployment and lower quality educational experiences, to name some of the most obvious.

Widespread infectious disease outbreaks, including coronaviruses, have affected human health for hundreds of thousands of years (Chapter 1). Late modern conditions such as globalisation have contributed to the rapid spread of new pathogens and rendered them risks that affect every part of the world. To counter this trend, however, expert knowledges developed as part of the conditions of late modernity are playing a major role in helping to control, treat and prevent COVID. A rapidly growing apparatus of expert knowledges has mapped the spread of SARS-CoV-2 and documented the efficacy of interventions such as vaccines and medical treatments. COVID is the first pandemic in which genomic sequencing has helped to identify viral variants, assist with contact tracing and determine patterns of spread.

Some of the contradictions that are part of reflexive modernisation and responses to risk in COVID societies are evident in social responses to vaccines against COVID. Effective anti-COVID vaccines have been developed and approved astonishingly quickly. However, the sheer unpredictability and complexity of how to control COVID in all its fast moving, continually mutating and highly infectious forms and modes of transmission pose a significant challenge to contemporary medicine and public health. The very acceleration of vaccine development has created doubt in some people's minds that they are safe. I noted in Chapter 2 that many countries, especially in the Global South, did not have adequate access to vaccines. However, even when supply improved as these vaccines were developed and rolled out, forms of vaccine hesitancy and resistance began to emerge.

These responses were often centred on understandings of risk that were multifaceted and context dependent. In some countries, in early to mid-2021, just as mass vaccination rollouts were beginning in many countries, alarmist news reporting focused on the serious but extremely rare side effects of some of the vaccines. For example, in Australia, headlines such as 'Six People Died During Pfizer Trial' misled readers (the vaccine did not cause these deaths) and a high level of news media attention was devoted to the blood clotting condition that affected a very small number of people who had received the AstraZeneca vaccine (Muller, 2021). Due largely to these news reports, Australians became increasingly hesitant about coming forward for a vaccine when they were eligible, citing concerns about side effects as the main reason.

A different set of circumstances in India meant that fewer than 3% of Indians had been vaccinated by mid-May 2021. While widespread vaccine shortages for such a huge population were one reason for these low levels of vaccination coverage, vaccine hesitancy and outright rejection were also major factors. In Mumbai slums in India during its devastating second wave of infection in mid-2021, many people adopted a fatalistic attitude to contracting COVID, viewing it as God's will, or were concerned that they may suffer side effects and not be granted time off work to recover. Others were worried that they would have to be tested for COVID before receiving a vaccine, and if found to be positive for the coronavirus would be forced into quarantine. Still others who were avoiding vaccination believed that COVID either did not exist or was not a serious disease. Social media were inundated with misinformation and conspiracy theories: including claims that COVID vaccines could make men impotent or that the vaccinations are ineffective or could even cause death themselves (Cohen, 2021).

Beck's ideas about individualisation and cosmopolitanism offer some insights in understanding the socioeconomic dimensions of risk responses to the COVID crisis. As shown in Chapters 2 and 3, many critical commentators have drawn attention to the failures of neoliberal democratic governments in managing the crisis. Instead of stepping in with appropriate social and economic support, many governments have relied on encouraging an approach to risk avoidance that aligns with Beck's ideas about individualisation. In terms of cosmopolitanism, the tensions and ambivalences Beck identified in his writings between feeling part of a global community but a tendency to return to nationalism when threatened are prominent in political responses to the pandemic. The very characterisation of the SARS-CoV-2 outbreak as a pandemic by WHO is itself acknowledgement that it is a risk that threatens the whole world. However, beyond broad statements about facing the risk as a global response from such health bodies, and important collaborations by experts across national borders in public health and medical science in efforts such as vaccine development, manufacture and distribution, most nations have retreated to nationalist sentiments and practices in their responses to managing and containing the spread of the novel coronavirus in their own jurisdictions.

Indeed, the intensification of nationalism is evidenced by many countries' leaders (across Europe and in the Australia Pacific region in particular) responding to the crisis by closing or tightening their international borders. In some cases, countries have even shut their internal borders when regions such as provinces, cities, local government areas or suburbs within cities or even individual apartment buildings have been 'ring-fenced' off from other regions (this has frequently occurred in Australia and China). The unseemly rush by national health authorities to secure vaccines and essential medical supplies such as respirators, therapeutic drugs and personal protective equipment for healthcare workers as the crisis disrupted global supply chains, even as low-income countries with escalating numbers of COVID cases and deaths and struggling healthcare systems were in greater need, is also stark evidence of pandemic nationalism.

Risk and sociocultural/symbolic theory

When Beck began his writing on risk society in the mid-1980s, a deadly new viral disease was spreading around the world: HIV/AIDS. While Beck did not mention this disease in *Risk Society*, the British anthropologist Mary Douglas was one of several cultural theorists writing about HIV/AIDS and risk in the 1980s and 1990s. Douglas also wrote about the cultural dimensions of risk more generally, with a particular focus on understanding why some people or social groups are identified as 'risky' and blamed for posing a threat to others. In her books specifically about risk – *Risk and Culture*, co-authored with political scientist Aaron Wildavsky (Douglas & Wildavsky, 1982), *Risk and Blame* (Douglas, 1992) and *Risk Acceptability According to the Social Sciences* (Douglas, 1985) – Douglas offers a social constructionist approach (Lupton, 2013). Like Beck, Douglas argues that the dangers and hazards that are labelled as 'risks' are real threats to human or planetary flourishing, but it is inevitably through the lens of social, political and cultural understandings that some phenomena are selected to be framed as risks while others are ignored or downplayed.

For Douglas (1992, p. 44), as well as Beck, 'risks are always political' and judgements of blame and attributions of responsibility are always part of risk politics and cultures. Douglas was less interested in social justice issues than was Beck, however. As an anthropologist, Douglas focused more than did Beck on the cultural specificities of risk understandings. Douglas adopted a cross-cultural perspective on risk understandings and practices, making frequent reference in her writings on risk not only to societies in the Global North (Beck's focus) but also to those in the Global South. Douglas adopted a functionalist perspective in trying to understand the classification systems and precepts by which societies maintain cohesion and social control. Douglas argued that all cultures have ways of dealing with anomalies that blurred symbolic boundaries, often treating them as dangerous and requiring control or exclusion.

In her initial work on purity and danger, Douglas (1966) observed that across diverse societies, ideas about phenomena or individuals who are considered anomalous, dirty or contaminating are culturally relative, dependent on the context in which they are established and reproduced. Building on these insights, Douglas (1985, 1992) and Douglas and Wildavsky (1982) developed an approach to risk that sought to identify how social groups, things and places are categorised in terms of their symbolic meanings and the ways they operate to demarcate Self from Other (both individually and collectively). Her cultural/symbolic approach to risk identified that ideas about the fleshly body and body politics are interrelated in casting blame on certain individuals and social groups for defiling the purity of a society.

In adopting this perspective, Douglas attempted to explain how people in specific contexts understand risk and what social and cultural purposes (or functions) are served by the rules and categories they follow. She argued that definitions and practices of risk are cultural strategies for these boundary markings and a way of dealing with social deviance and achieving social order. According to the cultural/symbolic perspective, people's concepts of risk are structured with and through their acculturation into specific historical and sociocultural contexts. Those phenomena that are perceived to be 'risks' or actions or things as 'risky' have changed over time and vary between societies and cultures. So too, ideas and practices related to the human body are situated and dynamic.

In Douglas' work on purity and danger, conceptually, the 'dirt' that requires control by societies can include viruses and other microbes that breach the boundaries both of the individual body and of the public body. In this context, people who are deemed Other are considered contaminated and carriers of the pathogens. As Douglas (1992) pointed out in relation to HIV/AIDS, people who are considered to be 'foreign' or part of outgroups who blur boundaries (such as gay men, sex workers or injecting drug users) are often blamed for spreading disease and are therefore treated with disgust, fear and a high level of surveillance and policing. These blaming mechanisms are integral to the ways that societies across history and globally manage the boundaries between Self and Other. Douglas' analysis of French people's concepts about the body and risk during the early years of the HIV/AIDS epidemic (Douglas, 1992) showed that the individual and the social body (the community) were considered permeable and vulnerable because they were viewed as 'too open'. It is notable that the centuries-old device of the cordon sanitaire – the protective physical barrier preventing infected outsiders from entering a space – was frequently evoked by these contemporary French people as the best way to keep out HIV.

A cultural/symbolic approach to risk can be employed to address such topics as news media coverage of infectious disease outbreaks and the types of outbreak narratives and pandemic imaginaries expressed in these accounts. The news media, including online outlets and social media forums, play an important role in framing novel health threats such as emerging infectious disease outbreaks and helping people make sense of what is happening and how concerned they should be about the threat. News media coverage is often a starting point at which people start to reflect on the seriousness of pandemic risk and its implications for their own lives (Davis & Lohm, 2020). However, news reports can also become hyperbolic, leading to scepticism and lack of trust in official sources or generating heightened feelings of fear, uncertainty, depression and anxiety (Davis et al., 2014).

Analyses of previous outbreaks have shown that discourses of moral panic, racism and victim-blaming have frequently appeared in news media coverage. Infectious disease outbreaks have been portrayed in the popular media differently, based on such factors as from what region or country they originated, the initial source of the microorganism and the manner by which it is transmitted from other animals or humans or from person to person. The Ebola virus disease epidemic, first emerging in 2013, was reported with particular tropes of fear, fascination, anxiety and disgust that was disproportionate to the number of lives it claimed. The 'primordial', 'swampy' rainforests of Africa were depicted as the risky spaces where humans and animals came together in 'primitive' ways (Wald, 2008, p. 7). In these portrayals, pre-established tropes of Africa and Africans as uncivilised and unhygienic frequently came into play, with the horrifying accounts of the high fevers and haemorrhagic bleeding that was part of the disease vividly portraying the leakiness of victims' bodies (Monson, 2017).

Naming of outbreaks by region (e.g. Spanish influenza, Asian influenza, Hong Kong influenza, Middle East Respiratory Syndrome) is one way that certain countries or geographical areas have been irrevocably, and often erroneously, associated with a pathogen and consequently subjected to moral judgement or blame for the outbreak, while the association of animals with the names of diseases (as in swine influenza and avian influenza) has stigmatised specific agricultural industries. It is for this reason, as well as for accuracy, that in 2015 WHO issued best practice guidelines for the naming of new human infectious diseases, emphasising that 'it is important that whoever first reports on a newly identified human disease uses an appropriate name that is scientifically sound and socially acceptable'. These new disease names should be based on the pathogen that causes it, the disease symptoms and if relevant its severity, seasonality, year of first identification or a specific age group it affects. The names should avoid the use of words that identify individuals, countries or geographical regions and that incite fear or panic (e.g. epidemic, unknown, fatal) (World Health Organization, 2015).

COVID and cultural/symbolic risk

Public representations of risk practices and risky people, including politicians' and health officials' speeches and press conferences, news coverage and public health campaigns, have made a major contribution to the ways that COVID risk has been framed. As discussed in previous chapters, certain social groups and individuals have been singled out for public attention as posing a threat to others because of actions deemed to be risky. As the novel coronavirus spread rapidly around the world, its invisibility and contagiousness led to fearful responses. People who became infectious were portrayed in the popular media and public health campaigns as lacking the good sense to protect themselves and posing a threat to others and to the healthcare system. Those who were accused of breaching public health orders – by not getting tested, failing to wear face masks or physically distance in public places, failing to stay in quarantine or isolation for as long as they should, travelling across borders, refusing vaccinations – were accused in the news media and by government officials as being selfish and dangerous to others.

The news and public health communication environment responding to the COVID crisis has been fraught, frequently characterised by conflicting or rapidly changing information as health authorities and governments struggled to make sense of this new outbreak and identify the best way to control its spread (Maher & Murphet, 2020). Some news outlets and social media platforms have been subjected to trenchant criticism for reporting or circulating misinformation, in what WHO has described as an 'infodemic' (Orso et al., 2020). The stereotyping, blaming and stigmatising of individuals and groups has also been a regular feature of outbreak narratives and pandemic imaginaries in news and online reporting globally. Ageism in social media content has been identified, with older people positioned as both more vulnerable and more expendable than other age groups (Meisner, 2021).

The metaphors that give meaning to the very new disease of COVID-19 draw on many of the same tropes that have provided humans with opportunities to express their feelings concerning illness, disease and death for centuries (Chapter 1). At the very beginning of the epidemic, the disease was framed in terms of a 'mystery' and a 'threat' posed by Chinese cultural practices: a disease of the Other, not of the Self (Lupton, 2021). Military metaphors have dominated, with constant references to the 'battle', 'fight' or 'war' against the 'deadly enemy' that is the novel coronavirus. There have more innumerable references to 'front line' workers, 'lockdowns' and 'heroes' such as medical and health authority personnel in news report after news report and in press conferences by politicians and health experts. One public health campaign run by the Australian government in mid-2021 even used the tagline 'Arm yourself against COVID-19' to encourage people to book in for a vaccination (punning on the visual image of arms ready for the jab and 'arming' as preparation for battle). Other metaphors have used extreme terminology to denote a sense of crisis, such as 'apocalypse' – a word originally from the Bible describing the end of the world. The implications of these metaphors are that citizens are expected to be fighting against the spread of SARS-CoV-2 and that those who already are infected have 'lost the battle' or indeed may have become part of the 'deadly threat' due to their contagious status.

Another Australian government advertisement running at the same time as the 'Arm yourself' campaign was designed to evoke fear tactics to shock young Australians into recognising that they were at risk from contracting COVID. Tag lined 'COVID-19 can affect anyone', the video showed a young woman in a hospital bed gasping for breath, panicked and looking around for help, with no visible sign of any healthcare professional offering it. There was a punitive dimension to these images of the terrified young woman. The clear message was that people who were complacent about COVID risk had only themselves to blame. Viewers were bluntly told to 'Stay home' and 'Book a vaccination' (even though at that time of the pandemic, vaccines were in short supply and not available yet to young people such as the woman depicted in the advertisement).

Racist discourses have featured in some news reporting, particularly against Chinese people, who have been frequently positioned as to blame for the emergence of the novel coronavirus in Wuhan (Wen et al., 2020). Due to widespread news media coverage of the novel coronavirus' origin in a part of China, people of Chinese ethnicity (or those who were judged by others to have Chinese ancestry) were targeted in racist attacks in many countries. In France in the early weeks of the pandemic, Chinese migrants and their descendants living in France were subjected to racist diatribes in the news and social media, including statements of blame for causing the outbreak due to their exotic eating habits and poor hygiene (Wang et al., 2021).

In the USA, former President Donald Trump continually referred to 'the Chinese virus' when discussing COVID and Asian Americans reported frequent incidences of hate speech and violence against them (Yellow Horse, 2021). During the first year of the COVID pandemic, Chinese students in the USA were faced with dealing with social stigma when wearing a face mask, as it marked them out as different, and potentially infectious, as well as a background of escalating political tensions between the USA and China, which contributed to anti-Chinese sentiment in the USA (Ma & Zhan, 2020). In the UK, people assumed to be Chinese were taunted with jibes and subjected to violent assaults. Some Britons refused to eat Chinese food, claiming fear of infection from allegedly poor hygiene practices from those working at the food outlet, and people of apparent Chinese appearance who wore masks in public were abused (Gao & Sai, 2021). In India, Chinese migrant communities living in the north-eastern region of the country were subjected to racist attacks and exclusion from public places, while Muslim minorities were openly exposed to bigotry from the government and subsequent hate crimes from other Indians (Rahman, 2020).

Discrimination and social exclusion internal to countries were also frequently demonstrated, based on assumptions about the threats that people in some communities or geographical areas posed to others. For example, within China, people who had contracted COVID and survived reported feeling being stigmatised, experiencing social rejection, financial insecurity, feelings of shame and social isolation (Yuan et al., 2021). In India, existing prejudices related to ethnicity, caste/class, skin colour and religion were heightened following the COVID outbreak. During the first national lockdown in response to COVID, poor rural migrants to the cities lost their jobs and were forced to travel long distances home on foot to their villages in mass numbers. They were offered no financial support by the Indian government. Nor was provision made for low caste or homeless people, large and highly vulnerable populations in Indian cities that was already exposed to high rates of violence, malnutrition and disease before the COVID outbreak. The Indian government appeared to be interested in controlling and monitoring these populations to protect others from the risk they posed rather than alleviating the harms to which these social groups were exposed as a consequence of COVID containment measures (Rahman, 2020).

An autoethnographic piece by an Indian academic Kishinchand Poornima Wasdani (2021) describes her experiences and those of her three young children as survivors of COVID living in an apartment complex in the Indian city of Bangalore. Wasdani recounts how she and her children were faced with significant social and mental health challenges: dealing with social isolation during lockdown, coping with stress, anxiety and fear when they received a COVID diagnosis followed by social stigmatisation and exclusion after they had been branded as COVID 'carriers'. Once Wasdani and her children had tested positive, a cordon sanitaire was put in place. Their apartment building was blocked off from the rest of the street, their apartment itself was sealed and red warning stickers were placed outside to warn others that COVID-positive people resided there. Rumours spread in the apartment building that the family was cursed, inflicted with coronavirus infection by God as punishment for imputed misdeeds. They were unable to receive food deliveries and were forced to live on whatever food was already stored in the apartment. When an old man who lived in the apartment died from causes other than COVID, the family was blamed and they were forced by other residents to keep their windows closed at all times, denying them fresh air. Even once Wasdani and her children had tested negative for the virus, their neighbours continued to shun them, and local shopkeepers refused to serve them. Other research has identified similar experiences and feelings of shame, guilt, social isolation and anger in people diagnosed with COVID in India (Sahoo et al., 2020) as well as in China (Liu & Liu, 2021) and Uganda (Amir, 2021).

In some national contexts, shaming, moral judgements and stigma were directed at people who were believed to have deliberately flouted public health orders. Countries such as Australia and New Zealand sought to control the ingress and spread of SARS-CoV-2 by erecting a cordon sanitaire around their international borders. Australia's international borders were closed early in the pandemic (March 2020) and the government maintained strong controls over the numbers of people who could enter or exit the country, to the point that it became very difficult to receive travel exemptions and visas even on humanitarian grounds. Within Australia, closing of internal borders between states and territories has often occurred as a way of preventing spread of the virus across the nation. The Australian news media has frequently identified people who failed to declare their infection status and crossed state boundaries or who had visited public places while infected, even when they did not yet know they were infected and therefore could not have been expected to have self-isolated. Maps showing places visited by such individuals were published in the news media, often accompanied by ridicule about the activities in which they had engaged or the sites they had attended. Some news outlets even published the names and photographs of these people and their family members at the top of their news feeds or on their front pages.

These border closures led to strong sentiments of nationalism, and what has been described as a 'Fortress Australia' mentality. This concept positions the country as a safe and uncontaminated space that must be protected from the ingress of infected outsiders, which even includes expatriate Australians who had been living overseas and were attempting to return home. Australians have expressed strong support for these measures. Most, simultaneously, have demonstrated little compassion for people who have been unable to leave the country to see family members who may be ill or dying or for Australian citizens who are stranded overseas with little support or in countries with high rates of COVID (Kassam, 2021).

In those countries where digital devices were used for close monitoring of people's movements and for determining whether they should be allowed out of quarantine or stay-at-home orders, people's identities were sometimes revealed publicly in a deliberate attempt to name and shame them as a warning to others. One such example involved a woman in China who was identified as COVID positive through health authority digital surveillance methods. Her name, full addresses and travel history were revealed in her local health authority's coronavirus updates and briefings. In the following days, other Chinese citizens engaged in a vendetta against her, finding as much online information about her as they could, including from her social media accounts, and republishing it, which were then disseminated in the news media. Public speculations were made about her personal relationship with another COVID-positive person who had been identified through digital surveillance, suggesting she was cheating on her boyfriend or was in a lesbian relationship. This kind of vendetta and news coverage involved gendered shaming, which sought to punish a woman for not ascribing to normative ideas of responsible feminine Chinese citizenship (Yu, 2020).

The concept of 'super spreaders' was used when the first SARS outbreak occurred. This phraseology referred to certain individuals who were singled out as highly contagious and therefore a risk to others: described in one media outlet as 'spewing germs out like teakettles' (Wald, 2008, p. 4). It reappeared in COVID news reporting and even in health authorities' accounts of people deemed to be 'hyper-infectious'. Events were characterised as 'super spreaders' as well, by virtue of the presence of one person who was themself characterised as a 'super spreader'. Thus, for example, an article on super-spreading events published on the prestigious *Nature* journal's website led with an example of a Christmas celebration held at a care home for older people in Belgium, in which 'the festive event … turned tragic' (Lewis, 2021). Forty staff members and more than 100 residents were infected by the person dressed up as Santa Claus, who visited without realising his COVID-positive status. The author goes on to note that:

> Superspreading events like this, in which many people are infected at once, typically by a single individual, are a now-familiar feature of the COVID-19 pandemic. Choir practices, funerals, family gatherings and gym classes have all spawned dangerous outbreaks.
>
> *Lewis, 2021*

These accounts emphasise the narrative of the 'ordinary' event turning into a disaster due to a hyper-infectious person who, despite their benign appearance (in this case, in the persona of Santa Claus) unwittingly, and invisibly, spreads contagion. The risk is heightened in this context, in which it is impossible to know who is a super spreader among those who might be infected.

The pejorative neologism 'covidiot' was also frequently used in social media discussions and news media coverage to describe people who were considered to have broken the rules and deliberately exposed others to risk. For example, a popular Indian-based Twitter news account, IndiaToday, with over 5 million followers, regularly posted videos purporting to show 'India's covidiot hotspots' – or regions of that country where cases were concentrated. One such video, posted on Twitter in July 2021, referred to 'the covidiot menace', people 'brazenly disobeying COVID norms', 'covidiots inviting a third wave', 'maskless tourists … condemned even by the Prime Minister' and 'massive social gatherings violating social distancing norms', with images of people being arrested by local police for attending such gatherings. Social media in India spread messages that contributed to the shaming of people with COVID infection, circulated the contact information or identities of such people and vilified them as 'super spreaders'. The shunning and stigmatising of people with coronavirus infection or even suspected of it was further exacerbated in some regions by government authorities' use of stickers on the gates of people's houses that identified them as confirmed COVID cases. Healthcare workers were also subjected to social discrimination and avoidance by others because of their assumed risky status due to close contact with infected patients. They became labelled as 'untouchables'. Some villages refused to allow cremation ceremonies for those who had died from COVID because of fear that their bodies would spread the virus (Joshi & Swarnakar, 2021).

Concluding comments

Ulrich Beck's risk society thesis comes together with Mary Douglas' ideas about Self, Otherness and danger in imaginaries and narratives of the emergence and rapid spread of SARS-CoV-2 and COVID. The risk discourses and practices circulating within and between regions and countries globally involve an affectively compelling combination of concepts of embodiment, contagion, danger and morality. They represent a wild and potent admixture of the threats and uncertainties generated by the combination of the old and the new, the primitive and the civilised, the local and the global. This very uncertainty, wrought by this new zoonotic pathogen, might be viewed as taking societies back to a pre-late modern era of risk: a time when, as I discussed in Chapter 1, plagues and other highly fatal infectious diseases regularly struck communities. The COVID crisis, then, can be considered both a pre-industrial, fateful event *and* a late modern risk society phenomenon. Chapter 5, taking up gender and queer theory, will show in more detail how ages-old ideas about bodily boundaries, the civilised body, the human subject and Self and Otherness have contributed to the COVID crisis but also how these ideas can be challenged.

References

Amir, K. (2021). COVID-19 and its related stigma: a qualitative study among survivors in Kampala, Uganda. *Stigma and Health*. https://psycnet.apa.org/record/2021-50259-001

Beck, U. (1992). *Risk Society: Towards a New Modernity*. Sage.

Beck, U. (1995). *Ecological Politics in an Age of Risk*. Polity Press.

Beck, U. (1999). *World Risk Society*. Polity Press.

Beck, U. (2004). *The Cosmopolitan Vision*. Polity Press.

Beck, U. (2009). *World at Risk*. Polity Press.

Cohen, J. (2021). Why is the world's largest COVID-19 vaccine campaign faltering? *Science*. www.sciencemag.org/news/2021/05/why-world-s-largest-covid-19-vaccine-campaign-faltering

Davis, M., & Lohm, D. (2020). *Pandemics, Publics, and Narrative*. Oxford University Press.

Davis, M., Lohm, D., Flowers, P., Waller, E., & Stephenson, N. (2014). "We became sceptics": fear and media hype in general public narrative on the advent of pandemic influenza. *Sociological Inquiry*, *84*(4), 499–518.

Douglas, M. (1966). *Purity and Danger: An Analysis of Concepts of Pollution and Taboo*. Routledge & Kegan Paul.

Douglas, M. (1985). *Risk Acceptability According the Social Sciences*. Russell Sage Foundation.

Douglas, M. (1992). *Risk and Blame: Essays in Cultural Theory*. Routledge.

Douglas, M., & Wildavsky, A. (1982). *Risk and Culture: An Essay on the Selection of Technological and Environmental Dangers*. University of California Press.

Gao, G., & Sai, L. (2021). Opposing the toxic apartheid: the painted veil of the COVID-19 pandemic, race and racism. *Gender, Work & Organization*, *28*(S1), 183–189.

Joshi, B., & Swarnakar, P. (2021). Staying away, staying alive: exploring risk and stigma of COVID-19 in the context of beliefs, actors and hierarchies in India. *Current Sociology*, *69*(4), 492–511.

Kassam, N. (2021). 'Fortress Australia': what are the costs of closing ourselves off to the world? *The Conversation*. https://theconversation.com/fortress-australia-what-are-the-costs-of-closing-ourselves-off-to-the-world-160612

Lewis, D. (2021). Superspreading drives the COVID pandemic – and it could help to tame it. *Nature.com*. www.nature.com/articles/d41586-021-00460-x

Liu, W., & Liu, J. (2021). Living with COVID-19: a phenomenological study of hospitalised patients involved in family cluster transmission. *BMJ Open*, *11*(2). http://bmjopen.bmj.com/content/11/2/e046128.abstract

Lupton, D. (2013). *Risk* (2nd ed.). Routledge.

Lupton, D. (2021). A 'mystery SARS-like illness'. How did Australian news outlets cover the COVID-19 outbreak when it first emerged in early 2020? *Medium*. https://deborahalupton.medium.com/its-been-a-year-since-the-first-australian-covid-19-cases-d7e4df44a550

Ma, Y., & Zhan, N. (2020). To mask or not to mask amid the COVID-19 pandemic: how Chinese students in America experience and cope with stigma. *Chinese Sociological Review*, online first. https://doi.org/10.1080/21620555.2020.1833712

Maher, R., & Murphet, B. (2020). Community engagement in Australia's COVID-19 communications response: learning lessons from the humanitarian sector. *Media International Australia*, *177*(1), 113–118.

Meisner, B. A. (2021). Are you OK, Boomer? Intensification of ageism and intergenerational tensions on social media amid COVID-19. *Leisure Sciences*, *43*(1–2), 56–61.

Monson, S. (2017). Ebola as African: American media discourses of panic and otherization. *Africa Today*, *63*(3), 3–27.
Muller, D. (2021). Alarmist reporting on COVID-19 will only heighten people's anxieties and drive vaccine hesitancy. *The Conversation*. https://theconversation.com/alarmist-reporting-on-covid-19-will-only-heighten-peoples-anxieties-and-drive-vaccine-hesitancy-161170
Orso, D., Federici, N., Copetti, R., Vetrugno, L., & Bove, T. (2020). Infodemic and the spread of fake news in the COVID-19-era. *European Journal of Emergency Medicine*, *27*, 327–328.
Rahman, S. Y. (2020). 'Social distancing' during COVID-19: the metaphors and politics of pandemic response in India. *Health Sociology Review*, *29*(2), 131–139.
Sahoo, S., Mehra, A., Suri, V., Malhotra, P., Yaddanapudi, L. N., Dutt Puri, G., & Grover, S. (2020). Lived experiences of the corona survivors (patients admitted in COVID wards): a narrative real-life documented summaries of internalized guilt, shame, stigma, anger. *Asian Journal of Psychiatry*, *53*. www.sciencedirect.com/science/article/pii/S1876201820302999
Wald, P. (2008). *Contagious: Cultures, Carriers, and the Outbreak Narrative*. Duke University Press.
Wang, S., Chen, X., Li, Y., Luu, C., Yan, R., & Madrisotti, F. (2021). 'I'm more afraid of racism than of the virus!': racism awareness and resistance among Chinese migrants and their descendants in France during the Covid-19 pandemic. *European Societies*, *23*(sup1), S721–S742.
Wasdani, K. P. (2021). Syndemic in a pandemic: an autoethnography of a COVID survivor. *Gender, Work & Organization*, *28*(S2), 605–611.
Wen, J., Aston, J., Liu, X., & Ying, T. (2020). Effects of misleading media coverage on public health crisis: a case of the 2019 novel coronavirus outbreak in China. *Anatolia*, *31*(2), 331–336.
World Health Organization. (2015). WHO issues best practices for naming new human infectious diseases. www.who.int/news/item/08-05-2015-who-issues-best-practices-for-naming-new-human-infectious-diseases
Yellow Horse, A. J. (2021). Anti-Asian racism, xenophobia and Asian American health during COVID-19. In D. Lupton & K. Willis (Eds.), *The COVID-19 Crisis* (pp. 195–206). Routledge.
Yu, A. (2020). Digital surveillance in post-coronavirus China: a feminist view on the price we pay. *Gender, Work & Organization*, *27*(5), 774–777.
Yuan, Y., Zhao, Y.-J., Zhang, Q.-E., Zhang, L., Cheung, T., Jackson, T., Jiang, G.-Q., & Xiang, Y.-T. (2021). COVID-19-related stigma and its sociodemographic correlates: a comparative study. *Globalization and Health*, *17*(1). https://doi.org/10.1186/s12992-021-00705-4

5
QUEERING COVID
Insights from gender and queer theory

Introduction

In previous chapters, I have drawn attention to the manifold ways that people living with socioeconomic disadvantage, people of colour, and those who depart from ideals and norms of behaviour have been marginalised, stigmatised or neglected during the COVID crisis. This chapter builds on and extend these findings by introducing insights from scholarship in gender and queer theory. Queer theory is now applied to a panoply of topics: what they share is a focus on challenging norms and providing different ways of seeing and doing identities and embodiments. To adopt a 'queer' approach is to focus on these dimensions of human (and in some cases, nonhuman) life. Underpinning applications of queer theory is a commitment to challenging traditional binaries such as those distinguishing between female/male, heterosexual/homosexual, human/animal and normal/deviant, acknowledging difference and supporting the diversity of identities and bodies and identifying and understanding the value of what lies in the liminal spaces between these categories.

Gender and queer theorists have critically analysed aspects of discourse, affect and embodiment to 'queer the pandemic': that is, to highlight disjunctures and invisibilities in the ways with which COVID has been portrayed and dealt and to provide further insights into the nature of lived experience in COVID societies. This scholarship therefore offers new ways of thinking through cultural representations, practices and affective responses to the COVID crisis. While contemporary queer theory has its roots in critical studies of gender and sexuality, it has since expanded well beyond these origins. There are many intersections and overlaps between gender and queer theory, and both reach into many related fields, including queer necropolitics, queer death studies, crip studies, fat studies and critical animal studies. These extensions of gender and queer theory and what they offer for analysis of the COVID crisis are considered in this chapter, drawing on the scholarship of Mel Chen, Michel Foucault, Judith Butler, Elizabeth Grosz, Gilles Deleuze, Félix Guattari and Julia Kristeva.

Gender and queer theory perspectives

Matters of life and death – and indeed, problematising the very definition of the animate and the inanimate, the human and the nonhuman – have long been central to queer studies. Ideas about the appropriate ways that people should present and conduct their bodies in response to dominant norms of behaviour are central to social lives and identities. As discussed in previous chapters, one of the most dominant logics organising ways of thinking and acting in contemporary societies in the Global North is that of the importance of engaging as a 'civilised' and responsible citizen to shape one's own life trajectory. As part of biopolitical beliefs about the importance of the civilised body, the care of the self and individualisation, people are constantly called upon by government authorities and health experts to engage in practices to control their lives and their bodies: including avoiding contracting or spreading disease and promoting their own health. These norms routinely position ideal contained bodies as young, male, heterosexual, able-bodied, lean and white. Bodies that do not conform to this ideal are continually marginalised and subject to discrimination, violence and neglect.

Contributors to gender and queer theory scholarship work to challenge these assumptions. Mel Chen (2012), a US queer and feminist theorist, points out that Eurocentric and species-centric approaches to biopolitics often exclude acknowledging those who are considered to be nonhuman or less-than-human. The 'civilised' human subject, in this representation, is an autonomous being who possesses and wields agency over others, adopts a rational approach to life and eschews dependence on other people or on nonhumans. People of colour, people with disabilities or chronic illnesses, fat people and other nonnormative bodies are often excluded from this definition.

In response, Chen (2012, p. 6) argues the case for bringing into biopolitical discussions such 'humanism's dirt' as nonhuman animals. Chen notes that nonhuman things are always part of the operations of biopolitics and biopower, including regimes of life and of killing.

Michel Foucault's writings on biopower, the role of discourse and expert knowledges in shaping understandings of bodies and the malleability of human embodiment in regimes of biopolitics have made a major contribution to gender and queer scholarship. As discussed in Chapter 3, Foucault positioned bodies as co-produced through discourses and practices as they operated together to respond to prevailing norms of bodily comportment. In his work, power relations were positioned as generating conditions of possibility in which bodies were formed and motivated towards movement and action. Foucault's perspective on contemporary relations of power viewed power as largely operating to encourage citizens to discipline and manage their own bodies through internalising authorities' advice and expectations rather than being coerced to do so.

Foucault's history of sexuality, a three-part set of volumes, has been highly influential in queer theory (Halperin, 1997; Spargo, 1999). Central to this work is Foucault's demonstration of how expert knowledges about sexuality have simultaneously operated to configure norms and bring nonnormative expressions of sexuality, such as homosexuality, into the light, rendering them more visible than ever before. Foucault himself identified as gay and contracted HIV/AIDS and died from the disease in 1984. His openness about his sexuality (if not his HIV-positive status) was an important factor in his influence in queer theory and activism: to the point that David Halperin, a gay historian, wrote a book about Foucault entitled *Saint Foucault: Towards a Gay Hagiography* (1997). Building on Foucault's scholarship as well as phenomenological insights into lived experience, gender and queer theory has turned towards a material-discursive approach that acknowledges the entanglements of language and symbolic meaning with embodied practices, affective forces and sensations.

Feminist theory has also been central to the development of queer theory by focusing on norms of gender. Writers contributing to analyses of gendered embodiment from a feminist perspective have drawn attention to the discursive and performative practices by which gender is established, made normative and maintained. They are interested in the phenomenology of gender and sexuality, or the lived experiences of 'doing' gender and sexuality. Feminist theorists have been in the forefront of identifying the ways in which human bodies can be thought about and treated differently. According to the scholarship of US philosopher Judith Butler (1988), performing gender and sexual identities is a continual and dynamic process rather than fixed in biological differences. Building on this insight, these practices can be open to transformation or subversion so that a multitude of gender and sexual identities can be performed. Bodies are born, but they are also made and remade over time. Bodies are shaped through gendered norms but can be reinvented in different forms, generating new and different practices of embodiment and identities. This is an affirmative approach to difference which acknowledges the importance of resistance and the capacity for change as part of constituting a broad spectrum of gender and sexual identities beyond normative binaries.

Feminist scholars have argued that in cultures of the Global North, male bodies tend to be considered far less permeable and more controlled than are bodies that are designated as female or other genders (genderqueer or nonbinary identities), which are culturally represented as leaky, chaotic and frequently out of control. As the Australian philosopher Elizabeth Grosz (1994) put it in the title of her book *Volatile Bodies: Towards a Corporeal Feminism*, women's bodies are positioned as 'volatile'. Grosz devotes attention in this book to the phenomenology of gendered bodies: what it is like to live in a gendered body. Building on Butler, Foucault and other gender and queer theorists, Grosz notes that bodies are inscriptive surfaces that are marked by the specificities of their existence. She describes the 'raw ingredients' out of which a body is produced as including 'its internal conditions of possibility, the history of its particular tastes, predilections, movements, habits, postures, gaits, and comportment' (Grosz, 1994, p. 142).

Grosz discusses the affective intensities and flows that move between human bodies, opening or closing capacities for action. This understanding of affect draws on the conceptualisation of French philosophers Gilles Deleuze and Félix Guattari. They described affects as productive and destructive forces that are composed with other affects and other bodies and therefore always shared and distributed forces (Deleuze & Guattari, 1987). Affective forces are also generated with nonhuman creatures and things. In their power and vibrancies, affective forces are integral to agencies, including more-than-human agencies. Affect from this perspective moves between human bodies. It includes, but is not limited to, emotion and embodied feelings and sensations. Deleuze and Guattari (1987) characterise affective forces as both affecting others and having the capacity to be affected.

Julia Kristeva (1982), a French feminist theorist, is another major influence for Grosz in her writing on gender and volatile bodies. Both Kristeva and Grosz were influenced by the work of Mary Douglas (Chapter 4) in considering the cultural and symbolic boundaries that are established in relation to the fleshy body and the body politic. In *Powers of Horror: An Essay on Abjection* (1982), Kristeva argued that bodies which are not considered 'clean' and 'proper' inspire feelings of abjection. The 'abject' is a phenomenon that is viewed as disgusting in relation to the orifices and boundaries of bodies. The process of abjection is part of the early development of the psyche, when children learn to distinguish their bodies from that of others: particularly their mothers. They must learn control over their bodies in terms of expelling waste. To do so, they learn to reject people and things that seem to transgress bodily boundaries, and which are thereby deemed to be abject. The affective responses of shame and disgust are part of the process of abjection, experienced first by young children when they are coming to terms with boundaries of selfhood and otherness. Abjection is repeated at the affective and psychoanalytic level throughout life as people continually work to establish their sense of selfhood and individuation. As Kristeva (1982, p. 4) puts it: 'It is thus not cleanliness or health that causes abjection but what disturbs identity, system, order'. This affective process is culturally contingent, as it relies on understandings of selfhood and embodiment that value individuation from others and from nonhuman things: predominantly a contemporary Western idea. It works to position some groups of people as less-than-human due to the ways that they are viewed as transgressing or blurring boundaries.

Some critical commentators have brought together necropolitics with queer theory, often also incorporating critical race and postcolonial theory. For example, US queer theorist Jasbir Puar (2018) has built on Mbembe's scholarship on necropolitics (Chapter 3) to describe 'queer necropolitics': the combined critique of violence against queer-identifying people combined with the queer community's complicity with Islamophobia after the 9/11 attacks on New York City. Puar suggests that the queer community often adopts a necropolitical stance in failing to acknowledge its own racism and exclusion of people of colour or those from religious minority groups from its sense of protected community. Similarly, in an overview of what they entitled 'queer death studies', Marietta Radomska, Tara Mehrabi and Nina Lykke (2020) describe this transdisciplinary area of scholarship as critically and affirmatively challenging conventional normativities and regimes of trust that give meaning to and emerge from necropolitics. They note that contemporary Western concepts of death, dying and mourning tend to ignore the necropolitical dimensions of the post-Enlightenment period, in which supposedly rational decisions were made to subjugate and inflict violence on women, people of colour and others who departed from the ideal of the 'civilised' body.

Queer death studies work to de-centre the privileged human subject as its focus, to 'de-exceptionalise human death' and to acknowledge people's relationships with and dependencies on other living creatures, objects, place and space (Radomska et al., 2020, p. 91). Queer death studies also intersect with critical animal studies (Taylor & Twine, 2014) in taking seriously the more-than-human dimensions of the current threats to human existence and well-being, such as climate change, species extinction and environmental degradation. In so doing, its purview extends well beyond that of conventional death studies, which tends to take the normative human body as its primary focus and rarely discusses topics relating to queer identities or the more-than-human dimensions of life and death (Radomska et al., 2020).

Queering disease and contagion

During the early years of the HIV/AIDS crisis, queer theory was crucially important in informing community and public health responses: including the work of activists and artists. An extensive body of literature has identified the moral meanings inherent in discourses and practices related to HIV/AIDS. As cultural and social analyses have identified, concepts of risk and of risk behaviours have frequently combined with discourses and practices that stigmatise those who are deemed to expose either themselves or others to HIV infection (see some earlier discussion of these issues in Chapter 4).

At the same time as HIV/AIDS began to spread around the world in the early 1980s, bringing with it a renewed spotlight on and stigmatisation of gay men's sexual practices, Foucault's scholarship was just beginning to make an impact in the Anglophone academic world. He became a pivotal figure not only in scholarly research on the socio-cultural and political dimensions of this new pandemic but also in community-led activism against the marginalisation of people with HIV/AIDS. Cultural scholars drew attention early on in the HIV/AIDS pandemic to what Simon Watney (1987) described as 'the spectacle of AIDS': the lurid tropes and images used to sensationalise HIV, the disease it caused, and the people who contracted the virus and died from it. US cultural theorist Paula Treichler's influential book *How to Have Theory in an Epidemic: Cultural Chronicles of AIDS* (1999) drew attention to the importance of gender and queer theory coming together with works of arts and acts of cultural resistance from the early days of the HIV/AIDS crisis. Building on Sontag's (1990) work on the metaphors of HIV/AIDS, in which she discusses the language of battle, invasion, victims, shame, guilt and Self and Other, Treichler (1999, p. 1) argued that the HIV/AIDS epidemic is also a 'semantic epidemic … an epidemic of signification' that is suffused with moral meanings. According to Treichler, analysing the language and discourse used to discuss HIV/AIDS is important because they shape how people with the infection or disease are treated by others, how they view themselves, what resources they are offered and to what extent they are protected or abandoned.

Cultural analyses showed that the bodies of gay men, injecting drug users, Black Africans and sex workers, to name the most prominent of the 'dangerous bodies' receiving attention in media coverage and other public discourses, were continually represented as more permeable to infection due to practices that were categorised as irresponsible, deviant or illegal. They were publicly vilified for their transgressive sexual or drug-using practices and blamed for 'deliberately' exposing themselves to the risk of HIV infection (Lupton, 1994; Treichler, 1999; Watney, 1987). Myths and conspiracy theories circulated that the origin of HIV was located in the deviant practices of Africans copulating with monkeys in the dense, remote jungles of Central Africa, or consuming contaminated monkey flesh, thereby allowing HIV into their bodies and starting the chain of transmission decades before the virus reached the Global North (Treichler, 1999). Such bodies were treated with abjection: considered leaky and unbounded, both due to their behaviours that were portrayed as inviting HIV into their bodies (through unprotected sexual activity or sharing needles to inject drugs) and their imputed contamination with HIV.

Instances abounded of people expressing fear about sharing the same space as these culturally polluting bodies, even after it was known that HIV was blood-borne not an airborne pathogen and could not be transmitted through touch alone. These affective responses were intensified by public health campaigns in the UK (the 'Don't Die of Ignorance' campaign) and Australia (the 'Grim Reaper' campaign) (Lupton, 1994) in the 1980s. These campaigns sought to stimulate feelings of vulnerability to HIV infection in majority social groups using horrifying images and metaphors of death such as gravestones and the Grim Reaper figure of death. The overall message of such campaigns was that everyone needed to be aware of the risk practices associated with HIV infection and to take steps to protect themselves from the apparent 'coming plague'. Unfortunately, the gruesome and frightening imagery and metaphors served to blame and stigmatise people with HIV/AIDS, evoking feelings of guilt, fear and shame (Slavin et al., 2007; Watney, 1987).

These portrayals, therefore, were highly normative and necropolitical. They marginalised or simply ignored the needs of people at risk from HIV infection or already living with HIV/AIDS: many of whom suffered and died while other people went about their everyday lives in ignorance of the severity of the outbreak and the grief and loss suffered by the communities who were affected. For HIV/AIDS activists and researchers, engaging with social and cultural theory offered a way of re-establishing a degree of agency as they battled to highlight the tragic deaths of people who became infected with HIV in the years when it was essentially a death sentence. It enabled them to identify and highlight the extreme forms of marginalisation, stigmatising and blaming that were targeting groups such as HIV-positive gay men, injecting drug users and sex workers as 'deserving sinners', while those who contracted HIV through blood transfusions were 'innocent victims' (Lupton, 1994; Watney, 1987). Activists and researchers formed networks of care and mobilised political action to demand better funding for medical care and research, and worked together to generate appropriate and effective information and prevention campaigns and strategies (Florêncio, 2020).

Once HIV/AIDS became a controllable disease in the Global North with the use of prophylactic and antiretroviral drugs, other health conditions began to receive attention in the news media, medical research and public health policy. From the late 1990s, these forums began to refer to an apparent 'obesity crisis' or 'obesity epidemic' that was described as sweeping the world and generating a 'burden' of disease and early death. There are now several decades of work in fat studies, an interdisciplinary area of studies that examines the discourses and practices that have led to and reinforced the pathologisation and stigmatisation of fat bodies in the wake of this intensified focus on the health risks associated with being fat. Scholars in fat studies have built on and extended the queering of dominant normative discourses about embodiment in critical approaches to HIV/AIDS. Due to the feminisation of fat bodies, feminist theory has been important to fat studies scholarship. Foucault's work on the care of the self in the context of neoliberal politics in healthcare systems has also been frequently taken up to queer the normative ideas of bodies that receive expression in anti-obesity discourses and practices (Lupton, 2018; S. Murray, 2008; Pausé et al., 2016).

Critical attention in fat studies has been paid to the ways that fat people are shamed and rendered abject by medical and public health discourses and practices, their abundant flesh portrayed as ugly, toxic and evidence of their greed and lack of self-control over their urges and emotions. Fat bodies are portrayed as leaky, abject and transgressive because of these assumed uncontained desires, but also because of their sheer physicality: their tendency to take up 'too much space' and therefore impose on other people's bodily boundaries (Lupton, 2018; S. Murray, 2008). These discourses and practices build on and intersect with neoliberal approaches to health that position citizens as responsible for taking control of their bodies so as to not to impose a financial burden on healthcare systems by becoming ill from 'lifestyle diseases' such as heart disease or diabetes. Such perspectives ignore the syndemic nature of such diseases and their social structural causes. Fat activists have responded to these discourses and practices by engaging in body positive activities that counter anti-obesity initiatives, acknowledge the diversity of body sizes and shapes and call for changes in the representation and support of fat people (Cooper, 2021; Pausé et al., 2016).

Similarly, cultural theorising concerning the bodies and identities of people living with disabilities now frequently uses the term 'crip theory' to distinguish itself. Crip theory is an extension of critical disability studies that devotes particular attention to queering dominant concepts of disabled embodiment. Scholars engaging with crip theory draw attention to the stigma, marginalisation and body shaming that is commonly directed at people with disabilities and those living with chronic illnesses or mental health challenges, as well as the materialities of their lived experiences. Drawing on Foucauldian theories of discourse and sexualities, crip theorists argue that just as heterosexuality has been historically portrayed as a 'nonidentity' that requires no declaration as it is assumed as the norm, so too, able-bodiedness is the normative category of embodiment that is positioned as 'the natural order of things' (McRuer, 2006, p. 1). Crip theory perspectives seek to detail the phenomenological dimensions of the types of nonnormative bodies that are often positioned in mainstream discourses and practices as inferior, abject, lacking or grotesque (Lajoie & Douglas, 2020).

In seeking to queer the distinction between human and nonhuman animals, contributors to critical animal studies provide a perspective on human health, disease, death and contagion that acknowledges the liminality of speciesism and challenges human exceptionalism. Scholars adopting a perspective that goes beyond anthropocentrism have pointed to the key role of multispecies relations in the management and control of infectious diseases that affect humans. For example, Celia Lowe (2010, p. 626) argued that H5N1 (avian influenza) in Indonesia emerged as a 'multispecies cloud' of humans, viruses, nonhuman animals (domestic poultry, wild birds and other creatures), resulting in a mass cull of chickens. She drew attention to the metaphorical, affective and material dimensions of these multispecies clouds in the geographical context of a climate in which humidity creates moist atmospheric clouds and a feeling of closeness and stickiness while anxieties focused on invisible aerosols and droplets moving in the air to convey the virus. An ethnographic account by Natalie Porter (2013) of avian influenza outbreaks as they were experienced and managed in Vietnam developed a biopolitical analysis that acknowledged that relations of biopower are not limited to a humanist focus. In the context of zoonotic diseases such as avian influenza, knowledges about human health and life intertwine with those about avian health and life. Veterinary expertise is equally as important as medical knowledge in an expanded public health system that encompasses multispecies entanglements. These initiatives are examples of the growing but unstable role of nonhuman animals in knowledges and practices related to human health and death (see Chapter 6 for further discussion of these issues).

COVID queering/queering COVID

The COVID crisis has itself queered human embodiment. Pre-COVID certainties, norms and expectations about how people should protect their health, interact with other people and with nonhuman animals and move in place and space have been disrupted. Ideas about the integrity of bodily boundaries and the types of bodies that are more permeable and open to the world have been challenged. Notions about intimacy have been overturned, as fears not only of touching others' potentially contagious bodies but of sharing the same air have circulated. As discussed in previous chapters, moral meanings have become assigned to such behaviours as someone leaving quarantine or physical isolation when they should stay away from others; not seeking COVID testing if they think that they may be infected; neglecting to engage in 'hand hygiene' or 'cough etiquette'; refusing to wear a face covering or to seek accept a vaccination and so on. SARS-CoV-2 itself has been portrayed as an invader of the body's boundaries. COVID control strategies insist on strict hygienic practices and mask wearing to scrub any viral particles from the body's surface or prevent them entering the orifices of the body. The openings of the body must be kept defended to be maintained as 'clean and proper'.

Broad analogies can be drawn between the blaming and shaming of people with HIV/AIDS and those who have COVID, but there are some key differences. While COVID-infected bodies are often portrayed in public discourses as abject in their contamination and threat they pose to others, these bodies are conceptualised as porous in different ways from HIV/AIDS-infected bodies. Infection is not associated with stigmatised activities such as male-to-male penetrative sex, paid sex or injecting drug use. COVID risk is instead inherent in banal everyday activities in which everyone usually engages. This is a key part of the difficulty of motivating and educating people to change the practices of a lifetime, such as standing close to people when interacting with them or shaking hands or hugging people when meeting. SARS-CoV-2 is far more easily transmitted than is HIV, meaning that anyone, from any age group or walk of life, can be a potential source of contagion simply by exhaling infected droplets or aerosols in the same space as infected people. The threat is far less visible or preventable, therefore.

Differences in experiences of temporality and spatiality have posed a challenge to many people during the pandemic, particularly in times of stay-at-home orders but also in relation to continuing uncertainties about what the future holds. Analyses of the experiences of people with disabilities or living with chronic illnesses have identified such phenomena as 'crip time', where temporal and spatial patterns are different from those experienced by many other people. During the pandemic, however, we are all living in 'crip time' (Thorneycroft & Nicholas, 2021). Everyone has found themselves confined to their homes and the possibilities for travelling beyond their neighbourhoods restricted. Everyday routines and normative life trajectories have been cancelled or postponed, resulting in the usual distinctions between work and leisure, home and work, weekend and weekday being blurred or dissolving (Moretti & Maturo, 2021). Rites of passage such as school and university final examinations, holidays and graduations and weddings have been disrupted. In these ways, expected norms, pathways and futures for people across a range of identities and socio-economic contexts have been 'queered' as old certainties have been problematised or upended.

Standard procedures that have supported late modern approaches to the control of health risks have also been queered by COVID. Throughout the COVID crisis, political leaders and government authorities have published 'road maps' or 'action plans' with various defined steps and often complicated rules and guidelines for controlling COVID and 'returning to normal'. Time and again, although they promise certainty, these plans and maps have been scrapped, completely reworked or forgotten, demonstrating that such approaches to crisis planning do not operate well in the fast-changing and highly complicated conditions of COVID societies. Previously accepted norms about safe spaces and borders have also been overturned again and again. For those countries such as the UK, China and Australia that have gone in and out of lockdowns (national, regional or local to the point of defined suburbs in one city) throughout the pandemic, each lockdown has had its own defined boundaries and rules that are different from previous lockdowns. Continuing border closures have led to spatial separations from intimate others that appear to have no end in sight. In these circumstances, public health advice about mobilities and spatialities have become ever-more fragile and open to contestation.

Long-held beliefs that socioeconomically advantaged people, particularly wealthy white men in the Global North, have held about the integrity and superiority of their bodies and health status have also been profoundly challenged. Death and the risk of severe illness or continuing disability due to long COVID symptoms have become much closer to these people, both in time and space. For the privileged few who are placed in the category of bodies that conform to normative expectations, death is often viewed as remote in temporal, social and geographical terms (Radomska et al., 2020). However, the COVID crisis, unlike any other catastrophe in recent times, has disrupted these norms and expectations. Assumptions about the safety of everyday practices and relationships have been shaken, while members of social groups that traditionally have been considered almost invulnerable to serious illness or early death have received public attention for becoming susceptible to and suffering from SARS-CoV-2 infection and disease. International celebrities (e.g. Tom Hanks, Kanye West, Marianne Faithfull, Madonna, Placido Domingo and Ellen DeGeneres) and elite world leaders, such as Donald Trump, Emmanuel Macron, Jair Bolsonaro and Boris Johnson, have publicly announced that they have tested positive to COVID. Johnson came close to death while spending a protracted period in intensive care and Trump was also hospitalised. Nonetheless, these people survived the disease, due at least in part to their access to the best possible healthcare and other benefits of their privileged lives. In contrast, just as gay men or Africans dying from HIV/AIDS were portrayed by news media accounts as expendable, not worthy of expressions of loss or grief, so too, the health and lives of racialised minorities in neoliberal democracies have been treated as expendable (Chapter 4).

Other marginalised bodies have also borne the brunt of body shaming and moral judgements during the COVID crisis. While anti-obesity discourses had receded somewhat at the time of the advent of the COVID crisis following a period of 10–15 years of intense news media and public health focus on the 'obesity epidemic' (Lupton, 2018), a renewed emphasis on the health risks of fat embodiment emerged during the COVID crisis, as medical studies began to be published that identified associations between body weight and COVID illness and deaths. Discourses of blame and moral judgements about lack of control began to receive attention in the news media, while fat people recounted further episodes of discrimination on the basis of their body size and appearance from healthcare workers and members of the public. As US-based fat activist blogger Aubrey Gordon observed: 'There has been an open debate about whether fat people [with COVID] are worth giving ventilators to, and I don't think we think enough about the impact of hearing the worth of your life debated in public'.

The UK government responded to this renewed attention to obesity by launching a new anti-COVID health campaign, the 'Better

Health Campaign', supported by Boris Johnson. In a video Johnson released to launch the campaign, he blamed his body weight for his severe COVID illness, stating that: 'When I went into ICU when I was really ill, I was way overweight … and, you know, I was too fat' (ABC News Online, 2020). The 'Better Health Campaign' had a strong focus on lifestyle change: not only losing weight if people were considered to be overweight or obese, but also giving up smoking, reducing alcohol consumption and engaging in higher levels of physical exercise. According to the campaign website, Britons were urged to 'kickstart your health' and that making changes to their everyday habits 'is easier than you think'. This campaign against 'the UK obesity epidemic' (ABC News Online, 2020) re-invigorated the self-responsibilised approach to weight control that characterised anti-obesity rhetoric during the 1990s and early 2000s that has been the subject of sustained trenchant criticism from fat studies scholars and fat activists for decades. In response, scholars and activists have called for attention to be paid to the social injustices and inequalities that the COVID has revealed and exacerbated rather than the continued emphasis on 'lifestyle change' that campaigns such as 'Better Health' promote (Cooper, 2021; Pausé et al., 2021).

The zoonotic dimensions of SARS-CoV-2 infection also introduce ways of thinking about contagion that inspire feelings of abjection based on blurring boundaries between the pristine human body and the contaminated animal body. Intimate relationships between human and other animal bodies, as evident in places such as farms and wet markets where humans routinely handle, care for and kill live animals, inspires feelings of abjection and disquiet if they appear to be 'unhygienic': mixing objects that should be separated, such as living and dead animals, or animal waste with freshly killed meat. Similarities in news reporting of the original SARS pandemic compared with COVID are evident in the focus on the conditions of emergence of both SARS pathogens as rooted in 'dirty' and 'primitive' conditions in which domesticated or wild animals and humans are in overly close contact. In the first SARS outbreak, farms in China were positioned as the sites of crossover of the virus to humans (Wald, 2008, p. 5). For the COVID pandemic, it was the wet markets in the large city of Wuhan which focused international media attention. The wet markets were depicted as bringing wild animals from their natural habitat into the metropolis where they were 'out of place', as Mary Douglas (1966) would put it, and therefore transgressive.

The imagined fluidities of the space of the wet market, blending the blood and other bodily fluids of humans and nonhuman animals in a location that is positioned as 'wet' because of both literal and metaphorical leakings, vividly outline the dangers of the liminalities that generate and pass on zoonotic pathogens. This characterisation is evident in an online news report on the suggested origin of SARS-CoV-2 in a Wuhan wet market published in the early months of the COVID outbreak. Prefacing his story with a 'graphic content' warning, the journalist wrote vividly of his disgust at images he had viewed of conditions in the wet market:

> Even for a carnivore like me, the images are gruesome and disgusting enough to consider whether I'll eat meat again. A smorgasbord of dogs being boiled alive, bats served on sticks like lollipops, kittens slaughtered, rats fried and giant snakes carved up for human consumption, with the blood splattering everywhere.
>
> *Wootton, 2020*

As this excerpt suggests, the imaginaries depicting certain places and spaces as contaminating and dirty, leaking pathogens, were translated to the animals and humans who occupied those spaces. The link between the racism experienced by Asian people living in other countries (Chapter 4) and the revulsion and Othering inspired by their animal consumption styles is exemplified in the piece. In the Global North, the people who work in conditions such as slaughterhouses, meat-processing and packing factories were among the most at-risk of contracting SARS-CoV-2 infection due to the spatialities and other conditions in their workplaces. This is a type of work that is marginalised and stigmatised because it involves intimate contact with the violence of killing animals and their bloodied flesh and viscera. These workers too were dehumanised by virtue of their abject status, with little concern about their working conditions or safety by their employers or government agencies (Oliver, 2021).

As scholars contributing to queer death studies and critical animal studies argue, most cultural analyses of death and dying are oriented towards humans. This anthropocentric priority is evident in the dominant portrayal of death, loss and grief in relation to COVID, which has focused squarely on human deaths. Yet millions of animals have also lost their lives in response to fears about their role in human loss of control over the novel coronavirus. In the process that is termed 'reverse zoonosis', humans can transmit viruses back to animals. This includes SARS-CoV-2, which humans have transmitted to mammals such as minks, rodents and felines such as tigers, pumas and lions held in zoos as well as domestic cats and dogs. This bi-directional capacity of zoonotic viral transmission means that risks to both humans and other animals are intensified. The virus mutates as it moves back and forth between their bodies, potentially evolving into more infectious strains that may be more resistant to current anti-COVID vaccines (Jia et al., 2021).

The mass culling of farmed mink that took place in Denmark in late 2020 involved the deaths of more than 15 million of these animals due to health authorities' concerns that a mutated form of the novel coronavirus found in the mink could hamper the effectiveness of COVID vaccines for humans. While Denmark is largest mink farming nation, with more than 1,000 mink farms, mink culls were also implemented in Spain, Sweden, Italy and the USA. In the case of the mink outbreak, it was humans who transmitted SARS-CoV-2 to the animals. A variant then developed in the mink that was passed back to a small number of humans (Jia et al., 2021; A. Murray, 2020).

The killing of nonhuman animals to protect humans against disease spread has many precedents. Mass slaughter of farmed pigs and fowl has featured in numerous previous zoonotic disease outbreaks as a blunt approach to protecting humans from the pathogens (Lowe, 2010). At the base of such apparently flagrant lack of concern for the value of the lives of these nonhuman animals is the overarching positioning of farmed mink as animals already destined for slaughter for their pelts, and swine and fowl as providing humans with eggs or meat. Their lives were already viewed by humans as worthy predominantly because of their economic value. In these approaches to nonhuman animals, a necropolitics that excludes the rights of these nonhuman animals is evident. Racist perspectives on the 'uncivilised' and 'unhygienic' practices of some Asian modes of farming and wild and domestic animal slaughter for human consumption are combined with blindness to the cruelty and disregard for animal welfare or the conditions of their lives that are typically part of Western modes of farming.

There are strong directions indicated in the material-discursive analyses of bodies outlined previously, which suggest how COVID embodiment can be 'queered'. Queer theory offers a way of rethinking notions of risk, safety and health in ways that do not always prioritise physical health over other forms of well-being. Such an approach to embodiment was a central element in HIV/AIDS activism, in which the importance of physical connection – sometimes involving unprotected high-risk sexual activity – was emphasised as a vital contribution to gay men's feelings of belonging, and therefore their well-being (Levina, 2020). The dominant discourse throughout the COVID crisis has been that bodies should stay a safe distance from each other to avoid potential virus carried in the air, and certainly not move close enough to touch, much less kiss, hug or engage in other forms of fleshy intimacy with other people. The idea that physical distancing could be achieved unproblematically, without provoking other consequences, was presented as a matter-of-fact mode of 'stopping the spread' in normative government and public health discourses and practices. A plethora of research studies have demonstrated the difficulties and costs of these exhortations to keep at a 'safe distance' from other people during the COVID crisis, including the 'touch' or 'connection hunger' that many people suffered when they were not able to touch other people (Durkin et al., 2021; J. Young et al., 2020). While video-calling and messaging apps and social media were widely used to meet people's needs for sociality and intimacy, these were still experienced as physically remote, tiring and a less satisfying mode of connection with others (Downing et al., 2021; Watson et al., 2021).

This focus on physical separation is a rationalist, privileged and disembodied figuring of the human body and of a 'dangerous intimacy' (Levina, 2020) that ignores the multisensory feelings, desires and other affective forces generated with and through people's interembodied connections with each other when they are sharing the same space. What is more, some people are placed in the invidious position of not being able to keep a safe distance, including those who must leave the house and engage face-to-face with others to earn an income in order to stay alive, including many people in precarious, low-paid or essential frontline work. Such individuals are routinely represented as irresponsible for not following public health orders, with little acknowledgement of the complexities and demands of their situation. Queering this discourse of safe-embodied encounters involves challenging the notion that people's longing and intense need for physical engagements with each other can be easily shut off, that all people are in a position to do this and that the boundaries of bodies should be closed as much as possible at all costs. It requires a more complex approach to public health than the antiquated and simplistic public health orders to physically distance and stay at home that have typically been issued by government leaders and health officials, along with threats and moral judgements concerning those who do not obey.

The insistence that people stay in their homes and only interact with other household members hit the queer community particularly hard, as it denied forms of queer sociality, identity and belonging. Many queer and LGBQTI people were faced with not only losing these affirmative connections and opportunity for kin-making and inhabiting safe spaces with community members but the uncertainty of knowing when they would resume (Trott, 2020). Restrictions about 'intimate partner' visits implemented by governments during lockdowns tended to assume a heterosexual relationship that was based on romantic ties. Echoing the kind of moralistic discourse that was so prominent in the early years of the HIV/AIDS pandemic, gay men who may have simply wanted a casual sexual encounter to fulfil their needs for sexual expression and intimacy were either ignored in such plans or castigated for not taking enough responsibility in protecting themselves or their sex partners from infection (Paceley et al., 2020; Philpot et al., 2021; Thorneycroft & Nicholas, 2021). Further, most appeals to people to 'stay home' assume a heteronormative family unit where household members have a secure and violence-free space to shelter from the danger posed by SARS-CoV-2 infection. As a consequence of all these factors, in some cases queer and LGBTQI people have experienced even greater challenges to their mental well-being than have other people, particularly feeling isolated or afraid of rejection or violence from those with whom they share a household (Paceley et al., 2020; Philpot et al., 2021).

Queer writers have emphasised the resonances of these experiences with queer communities living through the HIV/AIDS pandemic during its initial stages in the Global North. They have noted that with the onset of the HIV/AIDS crisis, gay men mourned not only the loss of friends and lovers but also their hard-won, and relatively new, freedom to engage in gay sexual activities actively and openly without fear or shame. The advent of HIV/AIDS returned gay sexuality to a world of pathologisation, with punishment of death. During COVID, these feelings of sadness and loss have resurfaced. Even though gay men and other queer-identifying people have not been specifically targeted as 'risky' groups, along with all other social groups they have become imbricated within new modes of self-responsibilisation and anxieties about passing on or contracting a serious disease (Levina, 2020; Philpot et al., 2021; Thorneycroft & Nicholas, 2021; Trott, 2020).

Nonetheless, having lived through the HIV/AIDS crisis or at the very least, possessing some cultural knowledge of it, has helped some queer people to mobilise and share resources, act as knowledge brokers for others and continue to contribute to community initiatives (Philpot et al., 2021). During the COVID crisis, and drawing on their long-established positive health communication activities, queer educators and activists have led the way in emphasising the importance of intimacy and sexual expression in the face of infectious disease and promoting safe ways of achieving these connections that limit viral infection (Florêncio, 2020; Levina, 2020; Pienaar et al., 2021).

Concluding comments

Throughout this chapter, I have discussed the manifold ways in which COVID has queered human embodiment. During the COVID crisis, new norms and expectations have come into play and new relationships and alliances have been generated. Moral judgements and feelings of abjection, however, are still generated in response to certain practices, relations and spatialities associated with specific modes of embodiment: many of which hark back to centuries-old notions of the integrity of bodies and the threat they pose to other people. Gender and queer scholarship demonstrate how nonnormative bodies and identities in the COVID crisis (and previous infectious disease outbreaks) have been positioned as less valuable and more contagious, abject, unbounded, contaminated or expendable than others. The abject body in COVID times is the person who fails to adhere to or flouts public health advice, thus inviting contagion into their own bodies and simultaneously placing others at risk by acting as a vector for the virus. In addition to identifying these cultural meanings and their implications for people's lives and identities, the process of queering COVID involves asking what it means to be 'at risk' or 'safe' and what are the wider stakes when some people are offered greater protection and safety than others and nonhuman animals' welfare is ignored? In considering how these responses might be subject to contestation and change, contributors to gender and queer scholarship imagine better and more inclusive futures. So too, scholars engaging with more-than-human theory expand their purview beyond the human subject by acknowledging the entanglements and mutual dependencies of humans with nonhuman agents. It is to these dimensions of COVID societies that Chapter 6 turns.

References

ABC News Online. (2020). Boris Johnson's Better Health campaign to tackle UK obesity epidemic. *ABC News Online*. www.abc.net.au/news/2020-07-28/boris-johnson-launches-strategies-to-tackle-obesity-epidemic/12497848
Butler, J. (1988). Performative acts and gender constitution: an essay in phenomenology and feminist theory. *Theatre Journal, 40*(4), 519–531.
Chen, M. Y. (2012). *Animacies: Biopolitics, Racial Mattering, and Queer Affect*. Duke University Press.
Cooper, C. (2021). *Fat Activism: A Radical Social Movement*. Intellect Books.
Deleuze, G., & Guattari, F. (1987). *A Thousand Plateaus: Schizophrenia and Capitalism* (B. Massumi, Trans.). University of Minnesota Press.
Douglas, M. (1966). *Purity and Danger: An Analysis of Concepts of Pollution and Taboo*. Routledge & Kegan Paul.
Downing, L., Marriott, H., & Lupton, D. (2021). "'Ninja' levels of focus": therapeutic holding environments and the affective atmospheres of telepsychology during the COVID-19 pandemic. *Emotion, Space and Society, 40*. https://doi.org/10.1016/j.emospa.2021.100824
Durkin, J., Jackson, D., & Usher, K. (2021). Touch in times of COVID-19: touch hunger hurts. *Journal of Clinical Nursing, 30*(1–2). https://onlinelibrary.wiley.com/doi/full/10.1111/jocn.15488
Florêncio, J. (2020). Writing theory during a pandemic. *Identities: Journal for Politics, Gender and Culture, 17*(1), 32–34.
Grosz, E. (1994). *Volatile Bodies: Toward a Corporeal Feminism*. Allen & Unwin.
Halperin, D. M. (1997). *Saint Foucault: Towards a Gay Hagiography*. Oxford Paperbacks.
Jia, P., Dai, S., Wu, T., & Yang, S. (2021). New approaches to anticipate the risk of reverse zoonosis. *Trends in Ecology & Evolution, 36*(7), 580–590.
Kristeva, J. (1982). *Powers of Horror: An Essay on Abjection*. Columbia University Press.
Lajoie, C., & Douglas, E. (2020). A crip queer dialogue on sickness. *Journal of Critical Phenomenology, 3*(2), 1–14.
Levina, M. (2020). Queering intimacy, six feet apart. *QED: A Journal in GLBTQ Worldmaking, 7*(3), 195–200.
Lowe, C. (2010). Viral clouds: becoming H5N1 in Indonesia. *Cultural Anthropology, 25*(4), 625–649.
Lupton, D. (1994). *Moral Threats and Dangerous Desires: AIDS in the News Media*. Taylor & Francis.
Lupton, D. (2018). *Fat* (2nd ed.). Routledge.

McRuer, R. (2006). *Crip Theory: Cultural Signs of Queerness and Disability*. NYU press.

Moretti, V., & Maturo, A. (2021). 'Unhome' sweet home: the construction of new normalities in Italy during COVID-19. In D. Lupton & K. Willis (Eds.), *The COVID-19 Crisis: Social Perspectives* (pp. 90–102). Routledge.

Murray, A. (2020). Coronavirus: Denmark shaken by cull of millions of mink. *BBC News*. www.bbc.com/news/world-europe-54890229

Murray, S. (2008). *The 'Fat' Female Body*. Palgrave Macmillan.

Oliver, C. (2021). Returning to 'the good life'? Chickens and chicken-keeping during COVID-19 in Britain. *Animal Studies Journal, 10*(1), 114–139.

Paceley, M. S., Okrey-Anderson, S., Fish, J. N., McInroy, L., & Lin, M. (2020). Beyond a shared experience: queer and trans youth navigating COVID-19. *Qualitative Social Work, 20*(1–2), 97–104.

Pausé, C., Parker, G., & Gray, L. (2021). Resisting the problematisation of fatness in COVID-19: in pursuit of health justice. *International Journal of Disaster Risk Reduction, 54*. www.sciencedirect.com/science/article/pii/S2212420920315235

Pausé, C., Wykes, J., & Murray, S. (2016). *Queering Fat Embodiment*. Routledge.

Philpot, S. P., Holt, M., Murphy, D., Haire, B., Prestage, G., Maher, L., Bavinton, B. R., Hammoud, M. A., Jin, F., & Bourne, A. (2021). Qualitative findings on the impact of COVID-19 restrictions on Australian gay and bisexual men: community belonging and mental well-being. *Qualitative Health Research, 31*(13), 2414–2425.

Pienaar, K., Flore, J., Power, J., & Murphy, D. (2021). Making publics in a pandemic: posthuman relationalities, 'viral' intimacies and COVID-19. *Health Sociology Review, 30*(3), 244–250.

Porter, N. (2013). Bird flu biopower: Strategies for multispecies coexistence in Việt Nam. *American Ethnologist, 40*(1), 132–148.

Puar, J. K. (2018). *Terrorist Assemblages: Homonationalism in Queer Times*. Duke University Press.

Radomska, M., Mehrabi, T., & Lykke, N. (2020). Queer death studies: death, dying and mourning from a queerfeminist perspective. *Australian Feminist Studies, 35*(104), 81–100.

Slavin, S., Batrouney, C., & Murphy, D. (2007). Fear appeals and treatment side-effects: an effective combination for HIV prevention? *AIDS Care, 19*(1), 130–137.

Sontag, S. (1990). *Illness as Metaphor and AIDS and Its Metaphors*. Anchor Books.

Spargo, T. (1999). *Foucault and Queer Theory*. Icon books.

Taylor, N., & Twine, R. (2014). *The Rise of Critical Animal Studies: From the Margins to the Centre*. Routledge.

Thorneycroft, R., & Nicholas, L. (2021). Queer and crip temporalities during COVID-19. In D. Lupton & K. Willis (Eds.), *The COVID-19 Crisis: Social Perspectives* (pp. 103–114). Routledge.

Treichler, P. A. (1999). *How to Have Theory in an Epidemic: Cultural Chronicles of AIDS*. Duke University Press.

Trott, B. (2020). Queer Berlin and the Covid-19 crisis: a politics of contact and ethics of care. *Interface, 12*(1), 88–108.
Wald, P. (2008). *Contagious: Cultures, Carriers, and the Outbreak Narrative*. Duke University Press.
Watney, S. (1987). The spectacle of AIDS. *October, 43*, 71–86.
Watson, A., Lupton, D., & Michael, M. (2021). Enacting intimacy and sociality at a distance in the COVID-19 crisis: the sociomaterialities of home-based communication technologies. *Media International Australia, 178*(1), 136–150.
Wootton, D. (2020). China's cruel wet markets that caused coronavirus and brought the world to its knees should be banned. *news.com.au*. www.news.com.au/lifestyle/health/health-problems/chinas-cruel-wet-markets-that-caused-coronavirus-and-brought-the-world-to-its-knees-should-be-banned/news-story/e92d62f2188361bec9079f105eb37699
Young, J., Pritchard, R., Nottle, C., & Banwell, H. (2020). Pets, touch, and COVID-19: health benefits from non-human touch through times of stress. *Journal of Behavioural Economics for Policy, 4*, 25–33.

6
MORE-THAN-HUMAN COVID WORLDS
Sociomaterial perspectives

Introduction

Given the intertwined dimensions of human and nonhuman relations and connections, the crushing impact of the COVID crisis extends well beyond human lives and agencies. A renewed interest in humans' relationships with things and places is evident across a range of humanities and social sciences disciplines and fields of academic research and scholarship. Scholars and researchers are beginning to engage with the body of scholarship that I refer to as 'more-than-human theory' (alternative terms used are 'new materialisms' or 'the critical posthumanities'). There are various varieties of more-than-human theory. In the discussion presented here, I focus specifically on the scholarship that builds on non-Western cosmologies (particularly Indigenous and First Nations philosophies) and the feminist materialism perspectives offered by Western philosophers Rosi Braidotti, Donna Haraway, Karen Barad and Jane Bennett. These philosophies advance a non-anthropocentric approach to understanding human existence. In recent years, scholars engaging with the more-than-human perspective advanced in these philosophies have made major contributions to identifying and considering the complexities of more-than-human existence, particularly in relation to the environment and human–animal relations: bringing together biopolitics with ecopolitics.

The implications of this approach for understanding the complexities of COVID societies are outlined in this chapter. More-than-human theory is applied to better understand the affective forces and relational connections that are generated with and through humans' encounters with nonhuman agents. I delve into the details of the assemblages of humans and nonhumans that have come together and come apart as the COVID crisis unfolded. As I show, such an approach expands the One Health perspective in productive ways. The discussion focuses particularly on how material things, including other living creatures, have contributed and been affected by humans' experiences, feelings and actions during the pandemic.

More-than-human theory

An important insight offered in more-than-human theory is that nonhuman entities are agential, generating liveliness and forces when they come together with each other and with humans. The concepts of 'human', 'life' and 'animate' are critiqued and expanded to include categories of entities beyond the narrow definition of human subject that has been privileged in post-Enlightenment Western thought (Chen, 2012; Grosz, 1994). Nonhumans include any of the agents that are part of the materialities of the planet: animals, plants, air, sun, wind and water, built and natural environments and all the objects that are part of these worlds. The concept of assemblage is also integral to more-than-human perspectives (Deleuze & Guattari, 1987). This term is used to denote collections or gatherings of humans and nonhuman agents that are situated in space and place but also dynamic as humans move through their everyday lives. A more-than-human perspective sees affective forces, connections and agential capacities as relational and distributed between the agents in human–nonhuman assemblages.

Indigenous, First Nations and other non-Western cosmologies reach much further back than contemporary more-than-human perspectives. These traditional philosophies of human embodiment and selfhood are traditionally more-than-human, contrasting with contemporary Western beliefs that tend to make a strong division between nature and culture, humans and nonhumans, and living and non-living things. These perspectives place great emphasis on the interembodiment of humans with other living creatures and the natural physical world in understanding the nature of human existence. These cosmologies view the nonhuman attributes of place and space as generating intense relational connections and affective forces with the humans who inhabit them. When these connections between people and nonhumans are disrupted or broken, illness and feelings of unease result that have negative impacts for humans and nonhumans alike (Hernández et al., 2021; Kwek, 2018; Rots, 2017; Smith et al., 2021; Todd, 2016).

For example, in Indigenous and First Nations philosophies, ways of knowing and learning are based in experiencing the complex more-than-human worlds through and with which humans move. This scholarship emphasises that the actions of recognising and making kin and tending to relations with nonhuman creatures and things should model caring and reciprocal forms of community. This involves being attentive to relatedness and connections in complex and ever-changing worlds. Such approaches are viewed as offering crucial insights into how the imbalances of human–nonhuman assemblages – and the violence and crises they create for human and planetary well-being – can be addressed and corrected (Hernández et al., 2021; Smith et al., 2021; Todd, 2016).

More recently, feminist materialism theorists have also made a major contribution to understanding the entanglements of humans and nonhumans. For scholars such as US philosophers Donna Haraway (2003, 2016), Jane Bennett (2009, 2010) and Karen Barad (2003, 2007) as well as Italian-Australian philosopher Rosi Braidotti (2019, 2020), forces and agencies are viewed as generated with and through human and nonhuman assemblages. Adopting a very similar stance to that originally put forward by Indigenous/ First Nations and other non-Western cosmologies, feminist materialism thought emphasises the intertwining relational connections between people and things. As Braidotti (2019, p. 1) writes; 'What or who is the human today can only be understood by incorporating the post-human and non-human dimensions'.

Feminist materialism scholars are interested in the micropolitical dimensions of more-than-human encounters and identifying in whose interests they serve. The notion that researchers should focus on 'how matter is made to matter', as Barad (2003) puts it, underpins much of this scholarship. An integral element of this understanding is identifying the affective forces that are generated in and through bodies, drawing on a Deleuzean understanding of affect as shared and distributed rather than inherent to individuals (Chapter 5). For Barad (2003, 2007), it is impossible to distinguish between ontologies, epistemologies and ethics, so she uses the term 'onto-ethico-epistemologies'. Her concept of 'intra-action' (as an alternative to 'interaction') also acknowledges the distributed and emergent nature of agencies and capacities. As Barad argues, rather than people and things interacting with each other and thereby exchanging or wielding agencies they already possess, they are viewed as 'intra-acting'. Through intra-acting, people and things together create new forms of agency and forces and in the process, become new entities. Haraway (2003) uses the term 'naturecultures' to encapsulate these entanglements and positions non-human living things as 'companion species' that live alongside and co-evolve with humans. Bennett's (2009) concept of 'thing-power' also recognises the vibrant affective forces generated by human/nonhuman assemblages.

For both Western and non-Western contributors to more-than-human perspectives therefore, agencies are viewed as never pre-existing or properties of actors (human or nonhuman). Rather, they come into being when assemblages gather, and as such, are motile and emergent rather than fixed (Hernández et al., 2021). These assemblages configure kinship (Haraway, 2016; Hernández et al., 2021) and thing-power (Bennett, 2004): forces that are dynamic and contingent on the time and space through and in which humans move, and the other humans, living creatures and objects with which they come into contact. Working together, humans and nonhumans generate agential capacities that can inspire and enact action, knowledge and other responses. This is an affirmative approach, which works towards understanding how much bodies are capable of as part of more-than-human assemblages (Braidotti, 2008, p. 32), acknowledging the temporal, spatial, affective and biographical coordinates of people's lives.

More-than-human contagion and spatialities

The embodied sensation of touch is central to understandings of contagion. The word 'contagion' is derived from the Latin *con* (with) and *tangere* (to touch). Its literal meaning therefore refers to touching other human bodies or things, and in doing so, becoming infected with a dangerous pathogen. As such, the 'immunitary impulse', as Lau (2016, p. 32) puts it, or alternatively the 'immunitarian mechanisms' described by Esposito (Chapter 3), operate to draw boundaries around people's individual bodies and the mass of bodies they are part of (households, social groups, citizens of nation states) so as to protect them from potentially infectious bodies (humans or animals) or objects, places or spaces and in some cases, water or air. Yet in a counter imaginary, immunity requires deliberate exposure to infective bodies or matter. The 'pure' body must allow entry to 'dirty' substances (pathogens or vaccines) in order to preserve its healthy status (Lau, 2016).

Social histories of medicine and public health have described how concepts and practices related to contagion, place and the humans and objects within those spaces are underpinned by broader discourses and beliefs about danger, risk and Otherness. In Chapter 4, I referred to cultural/symbolic understandings of risk and Otherness. I noted that material dimensions of people's lived experiences of risk and uncertainty include their multisensory and affective responses to space and place. Drawing on Mary Douglas' anthropological work on conceptual boundaries, risk and danger, I discussed the relationship between physical boundaries of place and space, fleshy boundaries of the human body and symbolic boundaries concerning protecting the integrity of the self and the community. As I noted, Douglas' scholarship on risk and danger emphasises the symbolic dimensions of materialities of contagion containment and the policing of boundaries in both literal and conceptual senses.

As discussed in Chapter 1, in the pre-modern era, quarantine practices became rituals for preventing pollution and maintaining cleanliness and immunity (both literal and metaphorical) (Bashford, 1998). Avoidance of foul vapours (miasmas) stemmed from a belief that bad smelling air somehow caused disease (Vigarello, 1990). Both approaches to contagion and disease control rely on spatial and sensory interventions. Expanding scientific knowledge about disease transmission, practices of disinfection, infectious disease surveillance and contact tracing emerged in the nineteenth century. In accordance with an intensified focus on the responsibilised citizen as part of biopolitical initiatives (described in Chapter 3), people were encouraged to take responsibility for hygienic practices in public and domestic spaces. Even before the role of bacteria and viruses in contagion was fully understood, researchers in science and medicine began to advise measures such as hand washing, disinfection of surfaces and face coverings to protect against infection (Mooney, 2015). The use of face masks for disease prevention has been traced back to the 1910–1911 Manchurian plague outbreak, following the emergence of new scientific knowledge that the pathogen could be airborne and breathed into the body (Lynteris, 2018).

In contemporary times, the One Health approach to public health and disease ecologies has emphasised the interrelationships and mutual dependencies of humans and other living organisms. Unlike the 'global health' approach, which remains a predominantly humanistic perspective, the One Health concept acknowledges nonhuman entities. Building on the ecological approach taken by the German public health pioneer Rudolf Virchow in the late nineteenth century, the term was originally coined by a veterinarian, demonstrating the role played by health experts on animals other than humans in the One Health concept (Wolf, 2015). The One Health approach has been viewed as a paradigm shift in medicine and public health by moving beyond a focus on the human body in a specific place and space to recognising the other living systems and ecologies in which diseases affecting humans are emplaced across the globe, as well as the interrelated nature of these systems and ecologies.

Other health sciences are also incorporated into the One Health perspective, including comparative medicine, environmental science, nursing science, plant pathology and biochemistry. It is notable, however, that beyond social medicine approaches, perspectives from the social sciences and humanities have not yet made a major contribution to the One Health approach, despite the importance of social changes such as globalisation, industrial agricultural systems, increased carbon emissions and mass international travel in influencing human, other animal and environmental health (Wolf, 2015).

More-than-human theory tends not to be included in the One Health literature, even though it highlights the dangerous or risky dimensions of multispecies relationships: particularly those enacted when pathogens that can cause serious illness or death enter human bodies by way of other animal vectors or hosts (Brown & Nading, 2019). While the interrelationships between humans and nonhuman animals are recognised in the concept of zoonotic disease, medical and public health thinking has often argued that 'spill overs' of microbes from animals to humans can and should be prevented as a way of protecting people from such infections (Marty & Jones, 2020). This assumption, frequently perpetuated in popular cultural representations of pandemics such as popular science books and science fiction, leans on the notions of the human species as separate from other species of living things and the contamination of humans by animals as a single event (Dey & Lynteris, 2021). It further relies on what medical historian Christos Lynteris describes as 'the fantasy that zoonotic transmission can be blocked or halted through techno-scientific intervention'. As he notes, this fantasy derives from late nineteenth-century beliefs about disease ecology which position contagious disease as spread by the practices of people of colour or those living in poverty (Dey & Lynteris, 2021, p. 178).

Just as it is important to identify how more-than-human assemblages contribute to feelings and practices of disease, discomfort and distress, current scholarship drawing on more-than-human theory in relation to health, illness and healthcare also often refers to assemblages of health, well-being and recovery. Such approaches have been adopted in medical geography and the sociology and anthropology of health and illness to explore how spatial and temporal dimensions interact in producing and reproducing the discourses and practices and, thus, the meanings and experiences of health, illness, and medical care. From these perspectives, feelings of health, well-being and recovery are performative and dynamic processes rather than complete events, a gathering of forces and agencies rather than a cognitive process located within the individual (Duff, 2016; Fullagar et al., 2019; Lupton, 2021). Contributors to this body of literature have called attention to the situated as well as globalised cultural discourses, beliefs and practices surrounding disease outbreaks and control. They demonstrate that the idea of One Health needs to recognise the multiplicities of specific contexts and historicities that are part of the vast entangled network of more-than-human health, including how multispecies encounters can contribute to human flourishing (Brown & Nading, 2019; Wolf, 2015).

More-than-human COVID assemblages

Viewed through a more-than-human lens, COVID risk concepts, experiences and practices can be conceptualised as assemblages of human and nonhuman agents that are continually coming together and splitting apart, generating affective forces that open or close off capacities for action. A more-than-human analysis can throw light on the multiple forces coming together in generating the COVID disaster and its catastrophic conditions. The sociomaterial dimensions of COVID risk span a plethora of entangled human and non-human agents: human bodies, the novel coronavirus SARS-CoV-2, the other animals involved in its transmission to humans, spaces and places of potential contagion, news reports, government policies and health campaigns, social media discussions, epidemiological data, modelling metrics and dashboards, quarantine facilities, face masks, soap and water, supermarkets, healthcare facilities, pharmaceuticals and vaccines ... and many more phenomena. More-than-human COVID assemblages are continually coming together and coming apart, their meanings founded in long-held beliefs and assumptions about cleanliness, immunity, danger and contamination and supported by an economic system that promotes continual consumption and commodification of objects and systems that offer feelings of safety and protection.

The sociomaterialities of air, breath and the ventilation of spaces have become central features of COVID risk discourses, as have the policies, objects and practices used to manage air flow. Some objects and spaces have been positioned as particularly 'unhygienic' because they are considered to harbour SARS-CoV-2 due to being potentially touched or coughed on by contaminated people: and therefore as requiring additional measures of avoidance or heightened efforts at cleaning. The novel coronavirus is transmitted from human to human by way of invisible viral particles (aerosols) emitted from infected people's air passages when they talk, laugh, cough, sneeze, sing, exercise or even just breathe heavily, that can float in the air and be breathed into the lungs of another person nearby, hatching another infection. The risk of infection is particularly heightened if people are sharing air in inside spaces with poor ventilation.

The materiality of this risk, coupled with its invisibility, has led to certain objects being figured as symbols of purity and hygiene. They can be either used to block viral particles from reaching the airways or mucous membranes in organs such as noses and eyes (face masks and the face shields and protective glasses used in medical settings) and touching human flesh (rubber gloves, surgical gowns and caps) or employed to scrub surfaces that may harbour contagion (soap, hand sanitiser, detergents). The level of obsession in some quarters with surface cleaning has been described as 'hygiene theatre' (Kale, 2021). It is undertaken for the sake of symbolically demonstrating that spaces and things are recuperated from their status as dirty/contaminated, even now that it is known that it is airborne viral particles that are most likely to infect people. Such obsessive attention paid to the cleaning of surfaces is a performative practice of safety that can intensify risk by diverting attention from the more difficult requirement to provide better ventilation in shared spaces so that SARS-CoV-2 is not as readily transmitted.

Certain consumer goods were invested with thing-power at various points in the pandemic, as assemblages of intense affective forces came together with materialities of production, distribution, supply chains, health advice, scarcity and commodification. Particularly in the early phase of stay-at-home restrictions imposed by governments, a behaviour that was typically described as 'panic buying' received high levels of attention in the news media in many countries. This phenomenon involved people rushing to supermarkets as soon as lockdown orders had been announced to strip the shelves of items such as toilet paper, hand sanitiser, tissues, paper towel, disposable face masks, soap, pasta and rice. People shared images of supermarket shelves that were empty, signs warning shoppers to buy limited numbers of items set by stores attempting to ration goods and long queues of people desperate to secure their toilet paper or other scarce goods. These behaviours, together with public discussion of them in mainstream news media and social media posts, highlighted the ways that ordinary domestic things that were once taken-for-granted – including the basic hygiene resource that is toilet paper – suddenly took on new symbolic meanings as rare and therefore extremely desirable commodities.

Face masks, simple and flimsy mass-produced objects that in most countries other than those in the East Asian region had previously not often seen outside hospitals and other clinical settings (Lupton et al., 2021), also became an integral part of everyday life in COVID societies across the world. Face masks provide a simple, low-tech barrier against the entry of airborne pathogens such as SARS-CoV-2 into the airways, and hence into the human body. From early in the pandemic, face masks were positioned as an important preventive agent against the transmission of SARS-CoV-2 but also were the subject of some controversy, as medical experts and authorities issued confusing messages about their efficacy.

Once it became largely accepted that mass masking could offer an inexpensive and effective measure to limit viral transmission, publics in most countries were encouraged to wear masks, particularly when in enclosed spaces or places where a safe distance from other people could not be maintained. In numerous jurisdictions across continents, mass masking was mandated in specific places, including schools, shops, public transport and workplaces. A thriving industry of handcrafted fabric masks emerged to meet the demand from publics for protective wear that was attractive, comfortable and re-usable, and therefore environmentally sustainable. Customised face masks could be ordered from online shopping outlets for any occasion: including Halloween, christenings and bar or bat mitzvahs, weddings, birthdays and funerals. For libertarians, however, mandated masking was viewed as an imposition on personal freedom, inspiring affects of anger and frustration that were vocally expressed in the organisation of public marches and rallies, especially in some parts of the USA (see Lupton et al., 2021 for more detailed discussion of the sociomaterialities and affective responses related to COVID face masks).

As the pandemic wore on, the image of the novel coronavirus itself became an instantly recognisable icon, emblazoned on t-shirts, posters and novelty socks as well as used repetitively in news reports. In the first COVID Christmas season at the end of the 2020, a range of COVID-themed Christmas decorations could be readily found online. These included tree baubles featuring images of Christmas icons such as Santa Claus or cute reindeer wearing face masks. SARS-CoV-2 icons appeared in Christmas-themed decorations (dubbed 'pandemic ornaments') for trees: in bright green and red hues, gold and glittery or grouped with other COVID iconic objects such as toilet rolls and face masks. Other COVID-customised decorations declared 2020 as 'The year we stayed home' or displayed the words 'Merry Christmas' together with a coronavirus symbol wearing a jolly Santa hat. Face masks could be obtained for wear at gatherings with Christmassy-themed patterns. Even COVID-themed Christmas stockings or sacks designed for holding gifts for young children were available for purchase.

As I have shown throughout the book, distinctions between Self and Other have continually been made during the COVID crisis, highlighting entanglements between material-discursive concepts of selfhood, the body and more-than-human assemblages. Both symbolic and literal borders have been established but have constantly changed as new 'hot spots' and risk groups have been identified. Some of these distinctions have been as broad as positioning whole countries or geographical regions and their citizens as contagious/contaminated and therefore to be avoided or subjected to having geographical borders closed to them. Other geographical borders distinguishing between 'safe' and 'dangerous' spaces have positioned the home or the neighbourhood as less risky than other spaces or contrasted safe suburbs with contagious suburbs even within the same city. Borders between these spaces have been closed and guarded so that people cannot exit or enter. Attributes such as the age, ethnicity/race or social class of the inhabitants of defined geographical spaces and assumptions made about their capacities to control their bodies and remain COVID-free have contributed to these discourses and practices.

Metaphors and other figures of speech have also contributed terminology that relates to the affective, spatial and multisensory intra-actions of human-COVID assemblages. The concepts of 'bubbles' or selective small groups of people with whom it is deemed 'safe' to interact and 'sheltering in place' both rely on language bringing together spatial metaphors with meanings suggesting protection. A bubble may be a fragile entity, but it is all-encompassing, yielding and malleable in its imputed protective capacities. A place that offers 'shelter' suggests a much more benign representation of spatial confinement than do the words 'lockdown' and 'isolation': both of which suggest carceral or punitive meanings.

In my research on Australians' experiences of the first six months of the COVID crisis, including a national lockdown (Lupton & Lewis, 2021a, 2021b), I found that people's feelings of risk or safety were closely related to spatiality and the inhabitants of place and space. Elements such as the initial news reporting of the COVID outbreak, feelings about observations of people located within the home or nearby (neighbours, the local community and local shopping areas) and environments such as people's gardens, the neighbourhood streetscapes and nearby parks were integral to how much they felt at risk and to what extent they managed to cope during the initial period of uncertainty and living through periods of physical isolation from others. Most participants had initially heard about the new viral outbreak through news reports and were aware that the first cases were reported in China: a place that Australians felt was a long way away and very different in terms of cultural practices and interactions. For some time, therefore, they viewed the outbreak as a distant threat that was unlikely to affect Australians. Even once the news media and government announcements made it clear that COVID was rapidly spreading within Australia, for those participants living in rural regions, the outbreak seemed even more remote from their everyday lives. They felt safe from contagion because they were distanced from crowds and had not heard of anyone nearby who had been infected.

Participants in my study also mentioned how they responded to other people when out in public. For some people, this was associated with particular spaces and the practices of other people in those places. People noted what others were doing and felt threatened or anxious by the apparent lack of care shown by some in not appropriately keeping a distance from others or failing to wear a mask. Supermarkets were singled out as particularly risky, and therefore anxiety-provoking, in these people's accounts. By contrast, the space of the home was considered by the participants as much safer because they felt in control of who could enter and spend time there. The inhabitants of their homes were predictable and known, unlike the strangers who populated and moved through public spaces.

In a very different geographical and cultural setting, a study based in the Mexican city of Monterrey in the early months of the pandemic (Meza-Palmeros, 2020) involving older women found that they articulated concepts of risk that related to their Catholic faith as well as the trust they invested in the President of Mexico as a political authority on public health matters. These women, nearly all of whom were already living with chronic illness and dealing with a precarious existence, recounted fatalistic concepts of risk or death from COVID. They were also aware of the risks of social isolation for their health and well-being. Similar to the Australians in my study, these Mexican women dealt with their feelings of vulnerability by positioning public places outside their neighbourhood as risky spaces. Their domestic and neighbourhood settings, although over-crowded, were viewed as less risky because they felt they could trust the other people in these spaces to not bring in infection.

Notwithstanding these feelings of safety within the home setting expressed by these Australian and Mexican people, they and many people across the world have felt imprisoned during COVID lockdown and restrictions periods, their autonomy for movement limited in unprecedented ways. A study involving interviews with young adults living in northern Italy at the time in which this region was the epicentre of the pandemic (early 2020) and subjected to severe stay-at-home orders found that these people were experiencing the space of the home in radically different ways compared with pre-COVID times. Temporal patterns had become disrupted, with weekdays blurring into weekends and working from home practices expanding into leisure time. Confinement within the home was viewed with ambivalence by these young Italians, with the home described as a refuge but also as suffocating, tedious and lonely (Moretti & Maturo, 2021). Further, as I discussed in previous chapters, some people, particularly women, children and LGBTQI people, have been exposed to greater violence during stay-at-home restrictions, which have forced them to spend long periods with violent family members. For displaced people, who may have left repressive political regimes and constant feelings of physical vulnerability to disease, violence and death, experiencing these feelings in their new, previously 'safe' country is confronting and unsettling (Mangrio et al., 2020).

More-than-human One Health and COVID

The One Health perspective can be readily applied to the COVID crisis. Indeed, several One Health exponents noted early in the COVID outbreak that this novel disease was a prime example of a One Health problem. For example, according to an editorial published in the journal *One Health* before SARS-CoV-2 had even spread beyond China, the viruses that are members of the coronavirus family (including SARS-CoV-2) are 'quintessential One Health viruses' because they affect both humans and other animals and are transmissible between humans and other animals (Marty & Jones, 2020).

Broadening from these types of simple observations concerning the zoonotic characteristics of the novel coronavirus, other commentators adopting a One Health perspective have drawn connections between the climate and biodiversity crisis to which humans have contributed: essentially positioning the emergence and spread of SARS-CoV-2 as the outcome of these environmental catastrophes (Garnier et al., 2020). These discourses position 'nature' as the victim of human malfeasance, requiring better protection and care from humans. Similarly, descriptions of wild animals reclaiming public spaces (albeit somewhat exaggerated or even invented, as in the case of the dolphins supposedly frolicking in Venice canals), or reductions in air pollution during periods of lockdown, portray 'nature' as recovering from the excesses and damages inflicted on it by humans.

These narratives offered a form of redemption, in which people were able to become aware of the possibilities for more-than-human relationships that would be benefit for all the creatures involved in the planetary ecosystem. By contrast, another oft-circulated idea that the pandemic was 'nature's way of fighting back' against a corrupted human species that had attempted to exert its will on other animals and living things. In this context, nature no longer depicted as a benign and benighted, if romanticised, entity, but rather as a forceful, vengeful agent of destruction, as embodied in SARS-CoV-2 and the disease and death it causes. This is the noxious side of nature, as represented by the plague and other devastating contagious diseases, which until recently was considered tamed and controlled by modern science and medicine. In these types of portrayals, they are imagined as emerging from the precursors to modernity – the kinds of human–animal relationships that were characteristic of the pre-Enlightenment era before 'civilised' and 'hygienic' practices that attempt to firmly delineate humans from nonhuman animals were instituted in the Global North.

As I noted in Chapter 1, there is a developing body of research on the importance of microorganisms in the human body for human health. We live with and through these colonies of microorganisms throughout our lives, sometimes suffering ill health as part of our intra-actions with these entities, but often experiencing mutually beneficial and supportive relationships and exchanges. To consider these microorganisms as 'inanimate' and as separate from us is not only reductive but misses many of the complexities of these multispecies ecologies: of which humans are simply one small part. A more-than-human perspective draws attention to the multispecies dimensions of the conditions of emergence and spread of SARS-CoV-2 as well as the impact of COVID. They further draw attention to the complexities of the concept of 'aliveness', sparking questions about how we might understand the novel coronavirus as animate. Viruses already occupy an ambiguous status in biological taxonomy. They are not considered living organisms because they are not made of cells, do not have the systems for metabolic functions and do not grow. However, once viruses enter the living cells of their animal or plant hosts, they become parasites on the metabolic systems of the hosts and can replicate themselves, directly exchanging genetic information with the hosts. Scientists first defined viruses as poisons (the Latin etymology of the word 'virus'), then as life forms and as biological chemicals, and more recently, as ambiguous entities that are somewhere between living and non-living (Villarreal, 2004).

Like all other microorganisms, viruses are our companion species, living with and co-evolving with humans as well as sometimes having mortal effects on our bodies. Despite the overwhelmingly negative portrayals of viruses – particularly when there are serious outbreaks that involve new and deadly pathogens – the vast majority of viruses live peacefully in human and other animal bodies. Most viruses do not cause illness or death in their hosts but can continue to replicate or lie dormant in the host's cells for long periods of time, avoiding detection by the host's immune system. Viruses can become part of the host species' genome and themselves are constantly changing and evolving as they rapidly replicate themselves (Villarreal, 2004). Genetic analysis has shown that tens of thousands of distinct viral species live in the human gut microbiome, feeding on the bacteria that are part of this teeming ecosystem but causing no harm to the human hosts, as they do not attack human cells. Viruses can even be used as part of phage therapy to attack harmful bacteria to prevent infections (Nayfach et al., 2021).

Adopting a more-than-human perspective on entities such as viruses, other microbes and any other agent that assembles with humans largely renders the debate about the liveness and agencies generated by viruses a moot point. Pandemics such as COVID starkly demonstrate how viruses can profoundly alter humans' way of life. As is common with most viruses, SARS-CoV-2 constantly changes its genetic form as it travels from host to host, generating a continual stream of variants that can be more virulent, contagious or resistant to current vaccines. The vitalities and sheer force of pathogens involved in pandemics such as COVID-19 as they shape and change human lives together with human bodies cannot be easily denied. The novel coronavirus intra-acts with human bodies in ways that may barely affect these bodies (if they are not infected or develop few symptoms). SARS-CoV-2 can make people seriously ill, killing them or causing long-term chronic health conditions as part of 'long COVID' symptoms. Beyond these physical effects on human bodies, the novel coronavirus has created vast social and economic upheavals and transformations in people's everyday routines and habits, as described in previous chapters. Intra-acting with humans, the virus has generated intense affective forces of fear, anxiety, dread and loneliness.

The language and discourse used to describe SARS-CoV-2 are revealing of its thing-power. As sociologists and anthropologists have argued, some pathogens can be characterised as 'charismatic', due to the sheer force and weight of the social and affective responses to them. Words and terms used in epidemiological language to describe the circulation of infectious diseases, such as 'spill over', 'jump', 'mutate' and 'colonise', position pathogens as forceful, agential and mobile (Herrick, 2019). SARS-Cov-2 is undoubtedly a charismatic microorganism. The metaphors describing COVID and SARS-CoV-2 drawing on hackneyed military terminology were discussed in Chapter 4. Related to this discourse, the novel coronavirus has been frequently anthropomorphised in descriptive language that positions it in human terms as a 'wily' and 'aggressive' 'opponent' that humans need to 'outsmart'. This language is exemplified in an article published in US online newspaper *The Seattle Times* (26 June 2020), in which readers are invited to see the world from the perspective of a virus such as SARS-CoV-2:

> Your goal is simple but wildly ambitious: invade and hijack the cells of a new host and multiply for as long it takes to establish your spawn in at least one other new host. Repeat until there are no humans left to infect ... Viruses are not as smart as humans, but they are much more patient.

Other portrayals of the coronavirus have depicted it as a criminal or murderer: 'You can always be stabbed in the back by a new variant', commented the Dutch caretaker Prime Minister Mark Rutte (Hawke, 2021). The undead monster – a zombie figuration – has also regularly appeared, as the coronavirus appears to be undefeatable, continuing re-emerging just when people have developed a sense of confidence that it is vanquished. This metaphor was evident in the words of an Australian academic quoted in a news story: 'We got ahead of ourself with opening up before we had put the last in the COVID coffin – and it lurched out' (Evans, 2021).

The choice of language to portray SARS-CoV-2 and COVID betray shared understandings and fears about contagion and the integrity of the body politic. In positioning the novel coronavirus as a fearful and cunning murderer or monstrous zombie, the military tropes appear justified and reasonable. What else but violence can work against this villain? Yet, as Sontag (1990) pointed out in her work on illness as metaphor (Chapter 1), the inevitable corollary of such portrayals is that the human bodies which harbour or spread the novel coronavirus or become ill or die from COVID can also become characterised as villains: or at the very least, as victims who have not fought hard enough or protected themselves well enough against infection and disease. Previous chapters have shown that this conceptualisation has permeated popular representations focused on Otherness, blame and moralisation.

In the context of the heightened affective atmospheres generated with and through human/nonhuman COVID assemblages, the thing-power of the vaccines that have been created to prevent severe disease caused by SARS-CoV-2 infection and transmission of the virus is intense. Vaccines are human-made agents, generated as part of a global knowledge network, diverse array of laboratory spaces and technologies, systematic approval and safety assurance mechanisms. The current range of COVID vaccines are remarkably effective in protecting vaccinated people (who have had at least two doses) against severe COVID and death from the disease as well as helping prevent transmission between people. COVID vaccines work in one of two ways. The first type uses modified versions of a different virus from SARS-CoV-2 that once entering the body in the vaccine generates a spike protein that can stimulate the body's immune system to create antibodies against the novel coronavirus (viral vector vaccine). The second approach involves mRNA vaccines, which train the body's cells to make this spike protein that triggers an immune response to SARS-CoV-2 (Centers for Disease Control and Prevention, 2021). Intra-acting with human bodies as part of the process of generating immunity to SARS-CoV-2, COVID vaccines also have a powerful role in limiting the agential capacity of the novel coronavirus not only to move between humans and therefore find more human hosts, but also to mutate and generate new variants that may be even more contagious than previous versions of the virus. The potent Delta variant that sparked new or worse outbreaks in many regions of the world in 2021, thereby prolonging the COVID crisis, is one such example of how unchecked replication of SARS-CoV-2 can have devastating and large-scale effects.

Across the globe, governments and health agencies are pinning their hopes on the agential capacities of the human-vaccine assemblage to bring a halt to the COVID crisis. Frequent references have been made to vaccines 'offering the best way out', 'offering hope' and even as 'a modern miracle'. There are multiple other agents and forces involved, however, that together intra-act with human bodies to either open up or close off capacities for protection from the worst effects of COVID. More-than-human vaccine systems include manufacturing capabilities, distribution systems and networks, appropriate storage facilities and voluntary licensing and technology transfer. These powerful agents all work with the pharmaceutical industry, itself a massive globalised industrial complex.

As noted in Chapter 2, the vaccine industry is highly political, and never more so than in the context of the COVID crisis. Forms of 'vaccine nationalism' on the part of wealthy nations' governments have hampered attempts by the governments of low-income countries to secure enough vaccine doses to provide adequate protection for their populations. Meanwhile, affective forces relating to fears about the risks of vaccines stemming from people's intra-actions with controversial media coverage and misinformation disseminated on social media platforms together with libertarian ideologies concerning people's right to refuse vaccines (Chapter 4) have swirled together in vibrant assemblages operating to close the vaccines' capacities to contain the spread of SARS-CoV-2, prevent the emergence of even more potent viral variants and protect human bodies against severe COVID.

Beyond recognising SARS-CoV-2 is a vibrant agent in humans' lives in COVID societies, it has become evident that other nonhumans have opened capacities for health, well-being and recovery from the devastation wrought by the crisis. As the COVID crisis worsened, news stories and social research findings began to appear that recognised the important part that people's relational connections with companion species played in their efforts to cope with the conditions of lockdowns and the continuing affects of anxiety, uncertainty, loneliness and dread that many people were experiencing. Reports of a surge in interest in adopting pets when people were in COVID lockdowns appeared across the globe (Ho et al., 2021). Research studies found practices such as chicken-keeping and gardening generated feelings of safety and comfort, allowing people to feel as if they are doing something to nourish other species and reconnect with nature (Oliver, 2021).

For the Australians in my research (Lupton & Lewis, 2022), companion animals were crucial contributors to their feelings of well-being during lockdown periods. In situations where people were starved of physical contact with other people, the opportunity to participate in an interembodied, multisensory encounter with another warm-blooded animal generated affective forces of companionship and affection. As one participant in my study observed, 'I'd be lost without my cat'. For those people who did not have direct access to other animals, sharing images of animals or remotely observing them in farms, zoos, animal sanctuaries or wildlife reserves using online live-streaming services became a popular way to find solace when they were feeling isolated and anxious: particularly during periods of lockdown (Turnbull et al., 2020).

These accounts of multispecies relational connections offer an affirmative perspective on more-than-human assemblages. Unlike the disregard for animal welfare evident in practices of mass culling of animals or the treatment of wild animals in wet markets (described in Chapter 5), people's accounts of the vital importance of their pets and other living things such as plant life in contributing to their well-being highlight the positive dimensions of blurred boundaries and intimacies with nonhuman creatures. In these contexts, human/nonhuman entanglements were able to generate affective forces of intimacy, relief and comfort, rather than the affects of disgust, fear and abjection that were evident in some other public portrayals of multispecies assemblages during the COVID crisis. This is an approach to more-than-human encounters that brings together care and responsiveness with an attunement to the nurturing vitalities that can be generated with agents beyond the human.

Concluding comments

I have shown in this chapter that more-than-human theoretical perspectives offer a way of highlighting the entanglements between humans and nonhuman agents that departs from the anthropocentric focus that often preoccupies social and cultural theory and research. The One Health perspective expands concepts and practices of biopolitics beyond the remit of the human body. In positioning nonhuman creatures largely as threats, it often fails to recognise the affective dimensions and mutual dependencies generated by human–animal encounters. A more-than-human perspective offers a deeper and broader perspective. These philosophies reach across millennia in drawing attention to the relational, dynamic, interwoven and non-linear dimensions of the intra-actions generated with and through human/nonhuman relations. Human authority and agency are decentred: replaced by recognition of the co-becomings with the multifarious creatures in more-than-human worlds and humans' attunement to their responsibilities to these creatures. More-than-human theorists often focus on the positive and beneficial relations shared by humans with nonhuman animals. They advocate for the importance of an ethical approach that promotes care for multispecies and views them as 'kin'. They emphasise that humans cannot be sequestered from other animals or other living things, as people are always already part of vibrant more-than-human assemblages – from the microorganisms that live in their guts or on their skins as part of their microbiomes to outwards into the environments they inhabit.

References

Barad, K. (2003). Posthumanist performativity: toward an understanding of how matter comes to matter. *Signs*, *28*(3), 801–831.
Barad, K. (2007). *Meeting the Universe Halfway: Quantum Physics and the Entanglement of Matter and Meaning*. Duke University Press.
Bashford, A. (1998). Quarantine and the imagining of the Australian nation. *Health*, *2*(4), 387–402.
Bennett, J. (2004). The force of things: steps toward an ecology of matter. *Political Theory*, *32*(3), 347–372.
Bennett, J. (2009). *Vibrant Matter: A Political Ecology of Things*. Duke University Press.
Bennett, J. (2010). A vitalist stopover on the way to a new materialism. In D. Coole & S. Frost (Eds.), *New Materialisms. Ontology, Agency and Politics* (pp. 47–69). Duke University Press.
Braidotti, R. (2008). Of poststructuralist ethics and nomadic subjects. In M. Düwell, C. Rehmann-Sutter, & D. Mieth (Eds.), *The Contingent Nature of Life: Bioethics and Limits of Human Existence* (pp. 25–36). Springer Netherlands.
Braidotti, R. (2019). *Posthuman Knowledge*. Polity.
Braidotti, R. (2020). "We" are in this together, but we are not one and the same. *Journal of Bioethical Inquiry*, *17*, 465–469.
Brown, H., & Nading, A. M. (2019). Introduction: human animal health in medical anthropology. *Medical Anthropology Quarterly*, *33*(1), 5–23.
Centers for Disease Control and Prevention. (2021). Different COVID-19 vaccines. www.cdc.gov/coronavirus/2019-ncov/vaccines/different-vaccines.html
Chen, M. Y. (2012). *Animacies: Biopolitics, Racial Mattering, and Queer Affect*. Duke University Press.
Deleuze, G., & Guattari, F. (1987). *A Thousand Plateaus: Schizophrenia and Capitalism* (B. Massumi, Trans.). University of Minnesota Press.
Dey, I., & Lynteris, C. (2021). On 'pandemic imaginary': an interview with Christos Lynteris. *Society and Culture in South Asia*, *7*(1), 175–180.
Duff, C. (2016). Atmospheres of recovery: assemblages of health. *Environment and Planning A*, *48*(1), 58–74.
Evans, S. (2021). What we've learnt about beating COVID. *The Canberra Times*. www.canberratimes.com.au/story/7343614/what-weve-learnt-about-beating-covid/?cs=14264
Fullagar, S., O'Brien, W., & Pavlidis, A. (2019). *Feminism and a Vital Politics of Depression and Recovery*. Palgrave Macmillan.
Garnier, J., Savic, S., Boriani, E., Bagnol, B., Häsler, B., & Kock, R. (2020). Helping to heal nature and ourselves through human-rights-based and gender-responsive One Health. *One Health Outlook*, *2*(1). https://doi.org/10.1186/s42522-020-00029-0
Grosz, E. (1994). *Volatile Bodies: Toward a Corporeal Feminism*. Allen & Unwin.

Haraway, D. (2003). *The Companion Species Manifesto: Dogs, People, and Significant Otherness*. Prickly Paradigm.

Haraway, D. (2016). *Staying With the Trouble: Making Kin in the Chthulucene*. Duke University Press.

Hawke, J. (2021). England will soon abandon almost all coronavirus restrictions. The Netherlands shows what could happen next. *ABC News Online*. www.abc.net.au/news/2021-07-18/freedom-day-looms-in-england-despite-coronavirus-surge/100295326

Hernández, K., Rubis, J. M., Theriault, N., Todd, Z., Mitchell, A., Country, B., Burarrwanga, L., Ganambarr, R., Ganambarr-Stubbs, M., & Ganambarr, B. (2021). The creatures collective: manifestings. *Environment and Planning E: Nature and Space*, *4*(3), 838–863.

Herrick, C. (2019). Geographic charisma and the potential energy of Ebola. *Sociology of Health & Illness*, *41*(8), 1488–1502.

Ho, J., Hussain, S., & Sparagano, O. (2021). Did the COVID-19 pandemic spark a public interest in pet adoption? *Frontiers in Veterinary Science*, *8*(444). www.frontiersin.org/article/10.3389/fvets.2021.647308

Kale, S. (2021). Hygiene theatre: how excessive cleaning gives us a false sense of security. www.theguardian.com/society/2021/jul/12/hygiene-theatre-how-excessive-cleaning-gives-us-a-false-sense-of-security

Kwek, D. H. (2018). The importance of being useless: a cross-cultural contribution to the new materialisms from Zhuangzi. *Theory, Culture & Society*, *35*(7–8), 21–48.

Lau, T. C. W. (2016). Defoe before immunity: a prophylactic *Journal of the Plague Year*. *Digital Defoe: Studies in Defoe & His Contemporaries*, *8*(1), 23–39.

Lupton, D. (2021). 'Things that matter': poetic inquiry and more-than-human health literacy. *Qualitative Research in Sport, Exercise and Health*, *13*(2), 267–282.

Lupton, D., & Lewis, S. (2021a). 'The day everything changed': Australians' COVID-19 risk narratives. *Journal of Risk Research*, online first. https://doi.org/10.1080/13669877.2021.1958045

Lupton, D., & Lewis, S. (2021b). Learning about COVID-19: a qualitative interview study of Australians' use of information sources. *BMC Public Health*, *21*(1). https://doi.org/10.1186/s12889-021-10743-7

Lupton, D., & Lewis, S. (2022). Coping with COVID-19: the sociomaterial dimensions of living with pre-existing mental health illness during the early stages of the coronavirus crisis. *Emotion, Space & Society*, *42*. https://doi.org/10.1016/j.emospa.2021.100860

Lupton, D., Southerton, C., Clark, M., & Watson, A. (2021). *The Face Mask in COVID Times: A Sociomaterial Analysis*. De Gruyter.

Lynteris, C. (2018). Plague masks: the visual emergence of anti-epidemic personal protection equipment. *Medical Anthropology*, *37*(6), 442–457.

Mangrio, E., Paul-Satyaseela, M., & Strange, M. (2020). Refugees in Sweden during the Covid-19 pandemic—the need for a new perspective on health and integration. *Frontiers in Public Health, 8.* www.frontiersin.org/article/10.3389/fpubh.2020.574334

Marty, A. M., & Jones, M. K. (2020). The novel Coronavirus (SARS-CoV-2) is a one health issue. *One Health, 9.* www.sciencedirect.com/science/article/pii/S235277142030015X

Meza-Palmeros, J. A. (2020). Risk perception, coronavirus and precariousness. A reflection on fieldwork under quarantine. *Health Sociology Review, 29*(2), 113–121.

Mooney, G. (2015). *Intrusive Interventions: Public Health, Domestic Space, and Infectious Disease Surveillance in England, 1840–1914* (Vol. 33). Boydell & Brewer.

Moretti, V., & Maturo, A. (2021). 'Unhome' sweet home: the construction of new normalities in Italy during COVID-19. In D. Lupton & K. Willis (Eds.), *The COVID-19 Crisis: Social Perspectives* (pp. 90–102). Routledge.

Nayfach, S., Páez-Espino, D., Call, L., Low, S. J., Sberro, H., Ivanova, N. N., Proal, A. D., Fischbach, M. A., Bhatt, A. S., Hugenholtz, P., & Kyrpides, N. C. (2021). Metagenomic compendium of 189,680 DNA viruses from the human gut microbiome. *Nature Microbiology.* https://doi.org/10.1038/s41564-021-00928-6

Oliver, C. (2021). Returning to 'the good life'? Chickens and chicken-keeping during COVID-19 in Britain. *Animal Studies Journal, 10*(1), 114–139.

Rots, A. P. (2017). *Shinto, Nature and Ideology in Contemporary Japan: Making Sacred Forests.* Bloomsbury Publishing.

Smith, A. S., Smith, N., Daley, L., Wright, S., & Hodge, P. (2021). Creation, destruction, and COVID-19: heeding the call of country, bringing things into balance. *Geographical Research, 59*(2), 160–168.

Sontag, S. (1990). *Illness as Metaphor and AIDS and Its Metaphors.* Anchor Books.

Todd, Z. (2016). An Indigenous feminist's take on the ontological turn: 'ontology' is just another word for colonialism. *Journal of Historical Sociology, 29*(1), 4–22.

Turnbull, J., Searle, A., & Adams, W. M. (2020). Quarantine encounters with digital animals: more-than-human geographies of lockdown life. *Journal of Environmental Media, 1*(2), 6.1–6.10.

Vigarello, G. (1990). *Concepts of Cleanliness: Changing Attitudes in France since the Middle Ages.* Cambridge University Press.

Villarreal, L. P. (2004). Are viruses alive? *Scientific American, 291*(6), 100–105.

Wolf, M. (2015). Is there really such a thing as "one health"? Thinking about a more than human world from the perspective of cultural anthropology. *Social Science & Medicine 129,* 5–11.

CONCLUSION
Reflections on COVID futures

We may not all currently 'live in the kingdom of the ill', as Sontag (1990, p. 3) described experiencing a cancer diagnosis, but we are all now living in the kingdom of COVID. Even if our individual fleshy bodies have not yet been infected with SARS-CoV-2 or perished from COVID, our bodies politic and our more-than-human worlds have borne the blows and bear the scars of the outbreak. This book has demonstrated the value of applying different sociocultural theoretical perspectives in explaining and understanding COVID societies. I have shown that we need theory more than ever. Indeed, we need a diverse range of theories that can elucidate the multiple, dynamic and intertwined dimensions of the continuing COVID crisis.

In the process of demonstrating how sociocultural theories can offer valuable conceptual insights into the complexities of the COVID-19 crisis, I have also provided an account of what it has been like to live through the first year and a half of this catastrophe across the world and the impacts the pandemic has wrought on social relationships and identities. Throughout the book, a series of intertwined threads have crossed back and forth between the macropolitical and micropolitical dimensions of COVID societies: contagion, death, risk, threat, uncertainty, fear, social inequalities, stigma, blame and power relations. Overarching these threads are five complementary themes: the historicity of COVID societies; the tension between local specificities and globalising forces; the control and management of human bodies; the boundary between Self and Other; and the continuously changing sociomaterial environments in which the world is living with and through the shocks of the COVID crisis. In moving back and forth between the minutiae of people's experiences of the COVID crisis and large-scale socioeconomic dimensions, between mundane practices and extreme levels of social disruption, disease and death, the book shows how interrelated individuals' lives are with the more-than-human relationships of which they are inextricably a part.

Across the world, across a multitude of diverse cultures and histories, people are suffering. They are vulnerable: to anxiety, fear, despair and insecurity about their future as well as poverty, ill-health and death. We think about our bodies and those of other people very differently these days. Touching other people and even sharing the same space and air have become acts not of conviviality, intimacy or companionship but instead have been positioned as potentially deadly practices that could spread disease between strangers and loved ones alike. The home has become a place of safety and shelter, protecting its inhabitants from the frighteningly invisible contagion that lies in wait outside; but simultaneously, it has been a prison, a lonely place, a space suffused with tension and despair, or for some people, marked by abuse or violence.

There are new forms of socialities in COVID societies. As people have become increasingly physically isolated from each other, ways of communicating using digital devices have come to the fore, involving novel ways of teaching, learning, working and socialising. However, the tolls of loneliness, disruption to everyday routines as well as the serious illness and death wrought by the rapid spread of the novel coronavirus have strained health services and generated widespread grief and dread. Most governments' responses to COVID control and management have involved fundamental challenges to people's freedoms: to move around in public spaces, access work or education, see family and friends, engage in leisure pursuits, take holidays, celebrate festivities and mourn at funerals. There is a major tension in balancing these restrictions with the potential harms they generate, such as poor mental health, widening gender and racial inequalities, exclusion from education, diminished access to healthcare and loss of income or exacerbation of poverty.

COVID societies call into question some long-established assumptions and return us in some ways to pre-Enlightenment times, when fate appeared to rule humans' lives. Together with becoming attuned to the other deep crises facing the planet – chief among them climate change and global warming – the COVID crisis has shaken core beliefs about the ability to control our destinies. At this point in the pandemic, people are reeling from the apparent lack of success that even the most powerful and wealthy nations have had in containing and managing its effects. Human societies have always faced crises and catastrophes, including recurring pandemics involving great misery, confinement and loss of life. These events have always inspired affective feelings of fear, anxiety and dread. They shake people's sense of safety and security and make them feel that their world has suddenly become an uncertain and unpredictable place. However, the COVID pandemic is the first truly global crisis since World War II.

For people living in disadvantaged, chaotic and dangerous situations or parts of the world, crisis is endemic rather than episodic: they are constantly in a state of fear and uncertainty, never knowing how their lives can be improved. What is remarkable about the current COVID crisis is that people in the Global North are now experiencing a prolonged crisis. Even for privileged social groups in high-income countries, the COVID crisis is continuing for far longer and has far broader impacts than any other previous crises or emergencies they have faced in their lifetimes. The current catastrophe challenges their norms and expectations about the security and safety of life and their futures and the control they can exert over their lives. COVID changed everything extremely quickly, but its impacts and dangers have not been easily resolved.

The major question for the future of the post-COVID world is 'What will "normality" look like?' once the crisis has passed or at least been dampened somewhat. It is difficult to determine yet whether the COVID crisis will lead to profound social and political changes; and if so, where in the world these transformations may occur. As I write, the crisis is continuing, and in some places, worsening. Uncertainties are proliferating rather than subsiding. The crisis has not yet become normalised or endemic. Even as we hope that things are getting better, we are still experiencing surges, outbreaks in new areas and emergencies, situations where apparent control has turned to sudden disorder. We do not know yet what the world will look like once COVID is better controlled. While hope was initially invested in the modern science expertise that developed and tested effective vaccines against COVID in record time, the continuing emergence of new, more infectious and deadly variants, together with breakdowns in the delivery of the vaccines have dented the initial optimism.

Governments and citizens just want everything to be over and to 'get back to normal life'. Many officials and politicians have made continual reference to the 'COVID normal' or 'new normal' state of affairs that they hope will eventuate. This goal, however, is apparently becoming less and less achievable. Instead, attempts to relax restrictions and becoming complacent about the threat posed by SARS-CoV-2 had time and time again led to loss of control over the virus. These terms assume a transformed kind of 'normal': one that will be marked forever by the events of the COVID disaster. It implies a new epoch in how everyday lives will be experienced post-COVID, potentially involving such practices as heightened awareness of personal hygiene measures and better ventilation to prevent infectious disease, less international air travel, working from home more often for those whose occupations allow it, the offering of more study online options, and an emptying out of the city and a population shift beyond the urban centres as a result.

Some health experts have suggested that the new normal may involve 'learning to live with COVID-19' by being alert to continued outbreaks, seeking regular booster vaccinations to counter the regular emergence of SARS-CoV-2 variants, self-isolating when exposed to the virus and engaging in other precautionary measures. They have speculated that rather than the COVID crisis 'ending', it will become endemic: a recurring threat like seasonal influenza. Such statements often lack nuance, however. They fail to recognise that 'living with COVID' will inevitably be a far better experience for the already privileged people who can readily find the vaccines they need, are in good health with excellent access to quality healthcare services and are able to maintain their levels of income during periods of stay-at-home or self-isolation restrictions. As societies 'open up', people living in conditions of socioeconomic disadvantage and social groups and populations who have been unable to access vaccinations will be facing a much higher risk of severe illness or death from COVID as well as even greater levels of debt, poverty or homelessness.

Beyond these practices, the 'new normal' phrase refers to an affective state of being. It suggests that people will begin to feel a sense of 'normality' again, which in turn is imbricated with feelings of hope, optimism, reassurance and well-being as compared with the affective states of anxiety, fear, powerlessness and uncertainty that have thus far characterised experiences of the COVID crisis for so many people. These kinds of pronouncements assume that most people are yearning for 'normality'. However, as I have shown in this book, normality in the pre-COVID world was experienced by many people as a state of entrenched socioeconomic disadvantage and marginalisation. Others, even those who were privileged, were struggling with prevailing feelings of dread and hopelessness about how pre-existing crises such as food insecurity, entrenched violence against women and climate change were affecting not only humans but all aspects of the planet. These people want a new normal that is very different from the 'old normal'. This imaginary of a 'better new normal' envisages a world where the neoliberal emphasis on 'small government' is wound back, the massive divides between the poor and the wealthy have been reduced, there is alleviation of poverty, the creation of stable employment opportunities and universal access to good quality and safe housing and healthcare. This vision looks beyond remediating the impact of the current COVID catastrophe to hoping that governments and global agencies would be making serious efforts to address the environmental effects of climate change and where preparations and investments for the continuing fight against further infectious disease outbreaks have been put in place.

Indigenous perspectives offer a way forward for recognition of nonhumans as kin as a way of achieving a better balance in more-than-human ecologies that will support both human and nonhuman flourishing. For Indigenous/First Nations thinkers, the COVID crisis inspired a chance to pause for a while and question the purpose of life, including recognising that humans cannot always be in control of or separate from nonhuman agents. The Yandarra research collective, including Australian Indigenous knowledge holders Aunty Shaa Smith and her daughter Neeyan Smith, together with non-Indigenous researchers Lara Daley, Sarah Wright and Paul Hodge, have interwoven local Indigenous storytelling with musing on the implications of the COVID crisis in offering ways forward for healing (Smith et al., 2021). In doing so, they acknowledge the violence wrought on the more-than-human world by colonialisation, but also map a path forward in undertaking the work that works with nonhuman agents to set things right and offer a chance to heal. The Yandarra collective notes that we cannot return to pre-COVID worlds. In facing the future, what is needed is greater recognition of how capacities for recovery in response to the devastation wrought by COVID can be generated. Central to this move towards promoting more-than-human flourishing is the recognition of human vulnerability. From this perspective, vulnerability is a vital affective force that opens capacities: 'Vulnerability is an important state for transformation. It pushes the boundaries of what is perceived and believed and enables us to let go of destructive patterns so that we can step into a field of creation' (Smith et al., 2021, p. 164).

As we step forward into creating a still uncertain post-COVID future, let us acknowledge our vulnerability and remember how intra-actions and relational connections with a variety of agents, not only other humans, have made us feel safer and more secure during these turbulent times. These are the relationships to hold to and protect, to give us comfort and relief from our suffering. They will help us become more open not only to the needs of our fellow humans but also to the more-than-human worlds of which we are always already a part.

References

Smith, A. S., Smith, N., Daley, L., Wright, S., & Hodge, P. (2021). Creation, destruction, and COVID-19: heeding the call of country, bringing things into balance. *Geographical Research*, *59*(2), 160–168.

Sontag, S. (1990). *Illness as Metaphor and AIDS and Its Metaphors*. Anchor Books.

INDEX

Note: page numbers in **bold** refer to tables.

9/11 attacks 106

Adhanom Ghebreyesus, Tedros 1, 76
affect: and embodiment 102; and socialities 10; understanding of 105, 126
affective forces 82, 105–106, 125–126, 130, 138–139, 141–142
affective state of being 149
affirmative biopolitics 63
Africa, Delta variant in 30
Agamben, Giorgio 10, 60, 64; 'bare life' 63, 70; on COVID 70–71; states of exception 63
AIDS *see* HIV/AIDS
Alipay 68
Amazon 47
'Arm yourself' campaign 94
Asian influenza **7**, 21
assemblage theory 125
AstraZeneca vaccine 88
Australia 28, 88, 141–142; 'COVID elimination' approach 46; digital privacy 69; 'Fortress Australia' mentality 97; 'Grim Reaper' campaign 109; international borders closure 96–97; public health campaign 94; quarantine practices 18; restrictive regulations 66–67
avian influenza **7**, 23, 92, 111

Barad, Karen 11, 124, 126, 127
'bare life' 63, 70, 72
Beck, Ulrich 10, 78, 82, 90, 99; on cosmopolitanism 84, 88–89; on individualisation 84, 88–89; late modernity, human-made threats 85; reflexive modernisation 83–84; risk society perspective 83, 99
'Better Health Campaign' 115
Bezos, Jeff 47
Biden, Joe 44, 45
'Big Pharma' 41
Bill and Melinda Gates Foundation 47
biopolitics, of COVID 59, 63; COVID testing rates 66; of death 64–65; digital technologies 68–70; governance of citizens 61–62; government regulations 66–67; immunity mechanisms 64; modes of power 60–61; necropolitics of COVID 73–77; social isolation measures 65; surveillance

Index

technology 68–69; technologies of the self 61, 62
biopower 9, 61, 62, 63, 78, 104
Bios: Biopolitics and Philosophy (Esposito) 63
bird flu *see* avian influenza
Birth of the Clinic (Foucault) 61
Black and Latino populations, social inequalities 50–51
Black Death *see* bubonic plague
'Black Lives Matter' protests 75
blame 85, 90, 92, 94, 109, 114
bodies 103; Butler views on 105; Foucault views on 104; Grosz views on 105; Kristeva views on 106
Bolsonaro, Jair 74, 75, 114
Braidotti, Rosi 11, 124, 126
Brazil 67; COVID deaths 3; 'hands off policy' 74–75
bubonic plague 16–17
Butler, Judith 10, 103, 105

capitalism 37, 38, 44
Chen, Mel 10, 103–104
China 29; atypical viral pneumonia in 26; COVID outbreak 29; digital surveillance methods 97; facial recognition systems 69; racist discourses against Chinese people 94–95; restrictive regulations 66; self-isolation restrictions 68; Wuhan pneumonia cluster 3, 26–28, 115, 116
Chinese Communist Party 66, 77
civilised body 15–16, 99, 103, 107
'Clarifications' (Agamben) 70
Clark, Helen 26
Coming Plague, The (Garrett) 22
contagion: imaginaries of 20; more-than-human 127–130; narratives 18; queering disease and 107–111; role 15; understandings of 127
Contagion (film) 22
coronaviruses: infections 14, 30, 65, 96; MERS/SARS 23, 25; spread of 49, 86, 87, 99; *see also* COVID-19; novel coronavirus (SARS-CoV-2)

cosmopolitanism 10, 83, 84, 86, 88–89
Cosmopolitan Vision, The (Beck) 83
COVID-19 25–26, 28; Agamben's views on 70–71; cultural/symbolic risk 93–99; deaths 3, 6, **7**; Delta variant of 29, 30, 49; Esposito's views on 71–73; first cases of 3; as lethal disease 25; material-discursive dimensions of 10–11; mortality 6, 7; naming 3; news media and 28–29; pandemic 1–2; political economy of 43–48; -related syndemic 53; research programme 4–5; risk society and 85–89; socioeconomic effects of 36; testing rates 66; vaccination programmes 3, 29–30, 65; *see also* coronaviruses; novel coronavirus (SARS-CoV-2)
COVID-19 Crisis: Social Perspectives, The (Lupton & Willis) 4
COVID crisis 2, 5, 8, 46, 47, 82, 99, 120, 147; biopolitical analyses of 65–70; economic effects 48; human societies 148; socioeconomic harms 54
'covidiot' 98
'COVID normal' 149
COVID queering 111, 120–121; COVID embodiment 117–118; 'crip time' phenomena 112–113; HIV/AIDS pandemic and 119–120; hygienic practices 112; LGBTQI people 119; obesity epidemic 114–115; physical distancing 118–119; pre-COVID norms 111–112; privileged lives and 113–114; reverse zoonosis 117; spatialities 112–113; wet market 115–116; zoonotic disease outbreaks 117
COVID societies 2, 8, 10, 15; disabled people in 52–53; futures of 11; historicity of 146; socialities in 147
COVID syndemic, social inequalities and 48–53

crip studies 103; *see also* critical disability studies
crip theory 10, 110–111
'crip time' phenomena 112–113
critical animal studies 10, 116–117
critical disability studies 9, 39, 52; *see also* crip studies
critical race theory 9, 39, 50; *see also* postcolonial theory
cultural/symbolic risk, COVID and: COVID-19 metaphors 93–94; digital surveillance methods 97; discrimination and social exclusion 95; public health campaigns 93; racist discourses against Chinese people 94–95; social stigmatisation 95–96; 'super spreaders' 97–98
Cuomo, Andrew 47

Daley, Lara 150
Defoe, Daniel 18
Deleuze, Gilles 10, 103, 105, 106
Delta variant of SARS-CoV-2 3, 29, 30, 48, 49, 67, 140
Dey, I. 5
Digital Health (Lupton) 4
digital privacy 69
digital technologies, for COVID surveillance 68–69, 70, 78, 97, 147
disability 39, 41, 52–53, 103, 113; *see also* critical disability studies
disaster capitalism 46–47
disciplinary power 9, 60–61, 62, 63, 67
Discipline and Punish (Foucault) 61
Douglas, Mary 10, 64, 78, 89, 99, 106, 115; 'cultural/symbolic' perspective 82, 83; on risk and danger 128; risk understandings 90–91; work on purity and danger 90, 91
Doyal, Lesley 40

Ebola virus disease 7, 23, 28, 92
Ecological Politics in an Age of Risk (Beck) 83
Engels, Frederick 37

epidemics, timeline of 7
Esposito, Roberto 10, 60, 71, 127; affirmative biopolitics 63; on COVID-related restrictions 72–73; on herd immunity 72–73; immunity mechanisms 64, 72

face masks: customised 132–133; for disease prevention 128
facial recognition systems 69
fat bodies 103, 109–110, 114–115
fat studies 10, 103, 109–110, 115
Fauci, Anthony 44
feminist theory 104, 110; *see also* gender
First Nations philosophies *see* Indigenous philosophies
Floyd, George 75
Food, the Body and the Self (Lupton) 4
Foucault, Michel 9–10, 59, 62, 64, 103, 107; on bodies 104; on care of the self 110; forms of power 60–61, 77, 78; Foucauldian theory 60, 83; gender and queer theory 104–105; history of sexuality 104; on medicine and public health 62–65; on micropolitics 62
France: coronavirus in 27; racist discourses against Chinese people 94
Freidson, Eliot 40

Garrett, Laurie 22
gender and queer theory scholarship 103; Butler on 105; Chen on 103–104; Deleuze on 105–106; Foucault on 104–105; Grosz on 105; Guattari on 105–106; Kristeva on 106; queer community 106; queer death studies 107
gender inequalities 51–52
gender theory 10, 99, 102–105, 108
German Ideology, The 37
global health 20, 26, 43, 129
globalisation 22, 37, 54, 87; benefits of 42; harmful effects on human health 42, 43; of risk 85, 86
Google 47

Index

Gordon, Aubrey 114
governmentality 61–63, 78, 83
government regulations 65–66, 71; in Australia 66–67; in China 66; in United Kingdom 67
'Grim Reaper' campaign 109
Grosz, Elizabeth 10, 103, 105, 106
grotesque body 16
Guardian, The (Honigsbaum) 67
Guattari, Félix 10, 103, 105–106

H1N1 outbreak 24
H5N1 23, 111
Halperin, David 104
Haraway, Donna 11, 124, 126, 127
Harvey, Gideon 17
healthcare 42; neoliberal approach to 77; system, in low-income countries 41; workers 27, 74, 75, 89, 99
Health Sociology Review (journal) 4
herd immunity 72–73
historical materialism 37, 60
HIV/AIDS 7, 8, 91; activists and researchers 109; COVID infection *vs.* 112; COVID queering and 119–120; cultural and social analyses 107–108; metaphors of 108; mortality rate 21, 22; queer theory and 107
Hodge, Paul 150
Homo Sacer: Sovereign Power and Bare Life (Agamben) 63
Hong Kong influenza 7, 21
Honigsbaum, Mark 67
Hot Zone, The (Preston) 22
How to Have Theory in an Epidemic: Cultural Chronicles of AIDS (Treichler) 108
'humoral' model 16

immune system 20, 21, 53, 137, 140
'immunitarian mechanisms' 127
Immunitas: The Protection and Negation of Life (Esposito) 63–64
Imperative of Health, The (Lupton) 4
Independent Panel for Pandemic Preparedness & Response 26, 31, 48

India 67; COVID cases 29, 49; racist attacks against Chinese 95; social media in 98–99; social stigmatisation, COVID people 95–96; vaccine shortages 88
IndiaToday 98
Indigenous philosophies 11, 124, 125, 126, 150
individualisation 83, 84, 88–89
Indonesia, H5N1 (avian influenza) in 111
infectious disease: outbreaks by region 92; vaccination programmes 20–21
influenza 25, 70, 92, 149; Asian 21; avian 23, 92, 111; Hong Kong 21, 92; Spanish influenza 5, 6, 9, 18, 19, 24; swine 24, 92
International Olympics Committee (IOC) 47, 48
'intra-action' concept 127
'Invention of an Epidemic, The' (Agamben) 70

Japan: coronavirus in 27, 30, 47–48; Summer Olympic and Paralympic Games (2021) 47
Johnson, Boris 44, 67, 114, 115
Journal of the Plague Year, A (Defoe) 18

Kristeva, Julia 10, 103, 106

Lau, T. C. W. 127
LGBTQI people 52, 74, 119, 135
life expectancy 40, 42, 74; Black–White gap 50; of Indigenous 41; Latinos 51
Lowe, Celia 111
Lykke, Nina 107
Lynteris, Christos 5, 129–130

Madness and Civilization (Foucault) 61
Marx, Karl 37, 38
Mbembe, Achille 10, 60, 73, 74; on biopolitics of death 64–65; scholarship on necropolitics 106
medical dominance 9, 37

medicalisation 73
Medicine as Culture (Lupton) 4
Medicine Under Capitalism (Navarro) 40
Mehrabi, Tara 107
MERS **7**, 23
MERS-CoV **7**, 23–24, 25
metaphor 16, 109, 134; of HIV/AIDS 108; military 93–94; plague 18; SARS-Cov-2 138–139
Mexico, COVID risk and 135
microbiome 20, 138, 142
microorganisms 17, 20, 137, 138
mink, culling of 117
Moderna 3, 47
moral judgements 82, 92, 96, 114, 120
Moral Threats and Dangerous Desires: AIDS in the News Media (Lupton) 4
more-than-human: contagion and spatialities 127–130; One Health and COVID 136–142; perspectives 142
more-than-human COVID assemblages 130–131; bubbles concept 134; COVID-customised decorations 133; COVID risk discourses 131; distinctions between Self and Other 133–134; face masks 132–133; 'panic buying' behaviours 132
more-than-human theory 124, 125–126, 130; One Health approach 129; 'onto-ethico-epistemologies' 127
mucormycosis 53
multispecies relationships 129

naming, of diseases 92
Nature (journal) 98
naturecultures 127
Navarro, Vicente 40
Necropolitics (Mbembe) 64
necropolitics of COVID 10; global health inequalities 74; global response to COVID 73; racial/ethnic minorities 74–75; shortages of supplies 75; stress, healthcare workers 75; vaccine distribution 76–77
neoliberalism 38–39, 42, 45, 54
New Public Health, The (Petersen & Lupton) 4
news media 4, 114, 132, 134; Australian 96–97; on infectious disease outbreaks 91–92; informing about COVID 28–29
New Zealand: cordon sanitaire 96; 'COVID elimination' approach 46
non-western philosophies 11, 124, 125, 127
novel coronavirus (SARS-CoV-2) 5, 7, 8, 14, 43, 112; cases/deaths 27–28; Delta variant 3–4; 'frontline' workers and 74; icons/images 133; infections of 3, 146; mink, culling of 117; mutations of 2, 86, 117, 138, 140; naming 3, 28; origin of pathogen 30–31; spread of 1, 3, 8–9, 25–31, 44, 52, 54, 87, 89, 93, 130–131, 136–139, 147; threat 86, 93, 149; vaccines 140–141; variants of 2, 25; in Wuhan 27–28, 94; zoonotic characteristics of 115, 136; *see also* coronaviruses; COVID-19

obesity epidemic 109–110, 114, 115
Olympic Games 30, 47
One Health (journal) 136
One Health approach 11, 125, 130, 136, 142; COVID vaccines 139–141; health sciences and 129; SARS-Cov-2 138–139; viruses 137–138
'onto-ethico-epistemologies' 127
Otherness 99, 106, 128, 139
outbreak narratives 5, 22, 91, 93

pandemic imaginaries 5, 91, 93
pandemic influenza ('swine flu') **7**, 23, 24
pandemics 24, 31, 41, 86, 138, 148; timeline of **7**; use of term 17
Pennell, Imogen 40

Index

people of colour 50–51, 64, 74, 75, 103, 106–107
People's Vaccine Alliance 76
pets 141–142
Pew Research Center 46
Pfizer 47, 88
pharmaceutical industry 3, 41, 43, 47, 76, 140
physical distancing 118–119
plague 16–17; literature 18; outbreaks, economic depression and 17; quarantine measures 17–18
Poland, geolocation tracking app 69
political economy of COVID-19 43–48; Australia 46; disaster capitalism 46–47; Japan 47–48; neoliberal 'small state' policies 45; New Zealand 46; Sweden 45; United Kingdom 44–45; United States 44, 45
Political Economy of Health, The (Doyal & Pennell) 40
political economy perspective 37, 39, 53; German Ideology 37–38; globalisation and 42–43; on medicine 40–43; neoliberalist policies 38–39, 42; postcolonial ideologies 41; public health and 40–43; socioeconomic factor 40–41; syndemic approach 41–42
Porter, Natalie 111
postcolonial theory 9, 39, 106; *see also* critical race theory
post-COVID 11, 148, 149, 151
power 77–78; biopower 61, 62; disciplinary 60–61, 62; as economic resource 38; forms of 9–10; modes of 60–62, 64; sovereign 60, 61
Powers of Horror: An Essay on Abjection (Kristeva) 106
Preston, Richard 22
Professional Dominance (Freidson) 40
Puar, Jasbir 106
public health: campaigns 42, 93, 94, 109; medicine and 62–65; political economy perspective 40–43

quarantine 16, 17–18, 65, 66, 68–69, 128
queer death studies 10, 103, 107, 116
queer necropolitics 10, 103, 106
queer theory 10, 102–104, 107, 117–118

racial/ethnic minorities, COVID necropolitics and 74–75
racism 41, 92, 106, 116; and colonialism 64; historical 50; structural causes of 39
Radomska, Marietta 107
Reagan, Ronald 38
reflexive modernisation 83–84, 87
reverse zoonosis 117
Risk (Lupton) 4
Risk Acceptability According to the Social Sciences (Douglas) 90
Risk and Blame (Douglas) 90
Risk and Culture (Douglas & Wildavsky) 90
Risk and Everyday Life (Tulloch & Lupton) 4
risks 82, 83, 90; Beck's definition of 84; cultural/symbolic approach to 91–92; cultures 10, 78, 82; governmentality 62, 63, 78, 83; sociocultural/symbolic theory and 89–92; theory 82, 83
Risk Society (Beck) 85, 89
risk society and COVID 10, 82, 99; anti-COVID vaccines 87–88; Beck's view on 84, 85; cosmopolitanism 88–89; COVID threat 86–87; ecological and environmental hazards 85–86; individualisation 88–89; intensification of nationalism 89; uncertainties 87
Risk Society: Towards a New Modernity (Beck) 83
Romeo and Juliet (Shakespeare) 18
Ruppel, A. 49
Russia, facial recognition systems 69
Rutte, Mark 139

Saint Foucault: Towards a Gay Hagiography (Halperin) 104

sanitary reform movement 19
SARS 7, 23, 27, 28, 29, 97, 115
SARS-CoV-1 7, 23, 25
SARS-CoV-2 *see* novel coronavirus (SARS-CoV-2)
Schaffer, S. 76
Seattle Times, The (2020) 139
self-care 61, 62
selfhood 61, 106, 125, 133
self-isolation 68, 69, 149
sexual behaviour 97, 104, 107–109, 112, 118, 119–120
Singer, Merrill 5, 41–42, 53
Sirleaf, Ellen Johnson 26
'small state' concept 38
Smith, Neeyan 150
Smith, Aunty Shaa 150
'social determinants of health' 37, 40
social discrimination, healthcare workers and 99
social inequalities, and COVID syndemic 37, 39, 48–53; Black and Latino populations 50–51; disabled people 52–53; gender and sexuality 51; in low- and middle-income countries 48–49; in United Kingdom 50; in United States 49–50; women 51–52
social isolation 65, 95, 96, 135
social stigmatisation, COVID people and 95–96
social suffering 77, 114
Sontag, Susan 16, 108, 139, 146
sovereign power 9, 60, 61, 63, 67, 78
Spanish influenza (1918–1919) 5, 7, 20, 24, 92; naming 18–19; pandemic 6, 7–8
spatiality 112, 113, 116, 120, 127, 134–136
states of exception 10, 63, 70
stigma 93, 95, 96, 99, 110, 112
'super spreaders' 97–98
surveillance technology 68–70, 78
Sweden, COVID-19 45
swine influenza 7, 24, 92
syndemic 5, 110; approach 41–42; COVID, social inequalities and 48–53

technologies of the self 61, 62, 68
Television, AIDS And Risk (Tulloch & Lupton) 4
Thailand: coronavirus in 27; vaccination programmes 30
Taiwan, vaccination programmes 30
Thatcher, Margaret 38
'thing-power' concept 127
touch 112, 118–119, 127
Treichler, Paula 108
Trump, Donald 44, 45, 66, 95, 114
Tunisia, coronavirus in 30
Twitter 98

Uganda, coronavirus in 30, 96
uncivilised body 15–16
United Kingdom (UK) 67; 'Better Health Campaign' 114–115; 'Don't Die of Ignorance' campaign 109; obesity epidemic 114–115; political economy of COVID-19 44–45; social inequalities in 50; violent assaults against Chinese 95
United States (USA) 27, 40, 67; anti-Chinese sentiment in 95; 'Black Lives Matter' protests 75; concepts of health in 19; COVID cases in 28–29; political economy of COVID-19 44, 45; social inequalities in 49–50

vaccines 3, 19; anti-COVID vaccines 117; AstraZeneca 88; COVID 29–30, 65, 87–88, 139–141; disparities in wealthy countries 76–77; distribution, politics of 76; for infectious disease 20–21; shortages 88; against viral infections 19
Vietnam: H5N1 (avian influenza) in 111; vaccination programmes 30
viruses 137–138
Virchow, Rudolf 129
Volatile Bodies: Towards a Corporeal Feminism (Grosz) 105
vulnerability 73, 109, 135–136, 150–151

Wald, P. 5
Walmart 47
Wasdani, Kishinchand Poornima 95–96
Watney, Simon 108
WeChat 68
wet markets 115–116
Whitty, Chris 36
Wildavsky, Aaron 90
women, COVID crisis and 51–52, 135
World at Risk (Beck) 83
World Bank 43
World Health Organization (WHO) 1, 6, 22, 26, 43, 76, 92; declaration of COVID outbreak 4; 'Global Strategy for Health For All by the Year 2000' 21; Health Emergencies Programme 24; infodemic 93; on Wuhan pneumonia cluster 27–28
world risk society 10, 83, 84, 86
World Risk Society (Beck) 83
World Trade Organization 43
Wright, Sarah 150
Wuhan, China 3, 26–28, 115, 116
Wuhan Institute of Virology 27
Wuhan Municipal Health Commission 26, 27

Yandarra research collective 150
Yoshihide Suga 48

Zika virus disease 7, 7, 23
zoonotic diseases 6, 43, 111, 115, 117, 129–130; *see also* reverse zoonosis

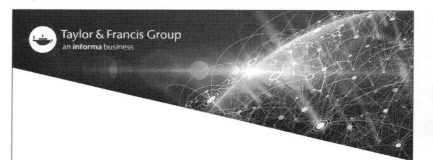

Printed in the United States
by Baker & Taylor Publisher Services